I0213656

Educating the Total Child

Educating the Total Child

Straight from My Heart

Six Decades of Guiding and Inspiring Children, Parents, and Teachers

Marvin Jacobson

Epigraph Books
Rhinebeck, NY

ISBN: 978-1-944037-39-0
Library of Congress Control Number: 2016945320

Epigraph Books
22 East Market Street, Suite 304
Rhinebeck, NY 12572
(845) 876.4861
www.epigraphps.com

Printed in the United States of America.

Table of Contents

DEDICATION

Educating the Total Child

I wish to dedicate *Educating the Total Child* to the memory of my parents, aunt and uncle, and son who supported me with their love and wisdom during the course of their lifetime.

Most importantly, my love and deep devotion goes to my wife, Lynn, who has worked beside me over the years as an educator and friend, and whose expertise was instrumental in establishing a curriculum that has stood the test of time and has continued into the new century.

To my daughter, Lauren, goes my appreciation and deep love, for carrying on my vision of the "Total Child" as current Head of Laurence School, and for continuing to improve and embellish on this learning environment that is so special. You are remarkable.

To Michael Wolke, father and pediatrician, for caring about the health and safety of all children. His expertise in diagnosing their health issues is admirable.

To my two wonderful grandchildren, Jonathan and Becky, I couldn't be more proud of you both for all that you have accomplished since you attended Laurence. I want you to know how much I enjoyed sharing the process with you from kindergarten through college. You have inspired me to keep dreaming for all these years.

To Alumni Parents Patti Claybourne, Janice Lang and Pat Orland, I thank you for your work organizing and editing these pages, as well as inspiring and helping me to move forward with my story.

This book is especially dedicated to:

- Parents who are continually trying to understand and seek out ways to help their children grow and thrive in a complex society
- Teachers who take it upon themselves to learn and adapt to the new theories and technologies that have defined the 21st century
- And of course...to children everywhere! I believe you are our future.

Foreword

The book you hold in your hands was written by a man who arguably knows as much as any living person about early education. Marvin Jacobson has worked as an educator since 1953, building one of the pre-eminent K–6 schools in the United States. In this domain, Mr. Jacobson may be fairly considered a national treasure.

Jacobson's concepts about the "Total Child," developed over time at Laurence School, served as the foundation for the education of generations of confident, optimistic, and capable children—children not only with polished academic skills, but young people of true character; students with considerable experience in critical thinking and the application of intellectual and moral judgment. It is this kind of education that prepares people to question assumptions and "think outside the box." In short, it is the kind of education that prepares one to *innovate.*

Empowering our children to innovate is likely to be the best assurance for continued economic security and personal fulfillment in a world of fierce competition and relentless uncertainty.

In *Educating the Total Child,* you will find the distilled lessons of more than a half-century of educating young people to stand tall and prevail in a world of breathtaking change. Like all fundamental truths, they will endure.

And they will support the dreams we dream for our children.

James H. Korris, Parent
President and CEO
Creative Technologies Inc.

PREFACE

I love children. I always have. Whenever I see a child smile and say "Good Morning, Mr. J" or "Hi" as he's passing through the campus, I feel happy. Nothing brightens my day more than a big hug and a friendly look in the eyes of a child.

I founded The Laurence School on my unwavering belief that education can enliven and strengthen the core of who we are—when we address and honor each child's physical, social, emotional, and academic development.

When asked what I attribute my success with children and families to, I say:

- *Passion* for youngsters, for learning, and the role of education in helping the "total child" grow.
- *Perseverance* in realizing my vision of families coming together to build and reinforce respect, responsibility, and caring and concern for others.
- *Patience* for all children and for teachers to appreciate the unique social and emotional needs that make each child special.

In the sixty plus years I have built, run, expanded, and grown the school. I have found that change is paramount to an institution's survival, growth, and continued excellence. I perceived this change not only as necessary, but also as an opportunity for optimism. Moving forward has allowed me to discover new things. In fact, the chance to go from "great" to "greater" gave me the courage to keep working, changing, learning, and creating new opportunities for children and their families.

I truly believe that first you dream and then you make it happen. *Straight From My Heart* is the story of my dream and my life's work. It is meant to be a resource for teachers, parents, and all those who strive to understand the skills, expertise, creativity, character, and cognition necessary to inspire and nurture young children so they can live and work successfully in today's rapidly evolving world.

I am so pleased to be able to share my thoughts with you on children, teaching, parenting, and the school I love.

Introduction

The correct way to educate the next generation, and the proper way to raise young children, has been a focus of study for many people and has resulted in a number of wide and varied practices throughout the ages.

Those who claimed to have found the "answer" presented their theories to the public first with hieroglyphics, then on papyrus, on paper, with the printing press, and now, today, they go viral on the Internet.

Some of these theories have turned out to be short-lived fads; some focused solely on the home, others entirely on the schools; most have not survived the test of time.

Initially the role of educating the child was primarily the purview of the parent in the home. As parents themselves have became better educated, and as both men and women have chosen careers outside of the home, schools have taken on a larger role.

Over sixty years ago, I started Laurence School with a new philosophy—one that partnered with the parents and focused on the "Total Child." This theory has stood the test of time and continues to raise young children who are confident in who they are, successful in later schools, motivated to serve others, and prepared for the future.

My premise is that children's development depends on their social, emotional, physical, and intellectual health. All of these aspects are intertwined, interdependent, and require support. Not one aspect can be successful alone, so it is important that parents and educators ensure a child's functioning as a whole.

I believe that the ultimate goal for us is to preserve, through the educational process, the beauty, joy, curiosity, and "what if?" that is innate within children. In addition, we need to teach our young not only the skills they need today, but also those which they'll need tomorrow—collaboration, critical and creative thinking, communication, public speaking, as well as the ability to adapt and use ever-developing technology in the pursuits of their goals.

I want to share the Total Child philosophy and educational goals with you in the pages of this book—how I used it to build a school, how you can use this philosophy in your parenting at home, and how educators can use this approach in their own schools. I am proud of my work, which started as a vision in a two-room schoolhouse and has grown to become a beacon for so many families who are looking for a solid educational foundation for their children sixty years later.

I still love young children and am excited by the educational opportunities that continue to fill the halls at Laurence. I am proud and happy to share my views and history with you.

Planting Seeds of Kindness

My Story

Everyone has a story.
First you dream,
Then you make it happen.

My story began when I started kindergarten in a small town in Westchester County, New York. When I had my fifth birthday, my mother took me to PS9, a small elementary school within walking distance from our home.

I was looking forward with great anticipation to going to school and learning about so many things that filled my head and senses with curiosity. What I wanted was to know more, and my thirst for knowledge was seemingly boundless.

As I entered the kindergarten classroom, I was immediately attracted to the book displays. I felt that my hunger for learning would finally be satisfied. I had so many areas of interest—the sun, moon, and stars; fables; how things work; why things are like they are; etc.—as well as questions to which I needed answers: What makes trains go fast? Why do flowers bloom in the spring? What does a President do? I discovered what I thought heaven might be like: a place to read, question, and learn. It didn't take long before my teacher, a dowdy schoolmarm, discovered, and was absolutely amazed by, her student who could read.

Her question was, how? My explanation was simple. When I went to the public library with my older sister, I was attracted to the children's section and began to look at picture books there. It fascinated me to find out what these pictures were all about. Soon I discovered that some books did not have any pictures, yet I could still find out their meaning. This excited me, and I relayed this to my teacher.

She accepted my explanation and assessed the situation as follows: "Marvin, you were self-taught." I replied (and I remember this clear as day), "I guess so." She continued with a scowl, "I don't really know what to do about teaching you since the other children are just learning their ABCs." From that moment on I felt that I was different from my classmates, and also that there was something fundamentally wrong with making a child feel this way!

Years later, as a college student, I chose psychology as my major interest, feeling particularly attracted to courses involving child development, which became my concentration. I understood from my days as a camp counselor how dynamic children are, each one different from the next. I also knew that they need to play, socialize, and develop their minds and bodies. Still, I wanted to learn more. So, during my early twenties, I volunteered in a Child Guidance Clinic and began to seek out mentors in the field. I was advised that if I was truly interested in working with children, the best way that I could understand them would be to teach them. The words still echo in my ears, "The best thing you can do is teach children." From that moment on, I believed my future would be in education and in the classroom.

This important recommendation, coupled with my own desire to know more, led me to enroll in UCLA's Graduate School of Education. The two years I spent there were incredibly instructive and involved much hands-on observation. I became a disciple of pre-eminent educators John Dewey, William Heard Kilpatrick, and Corinne Seeds, who at that time was the Principal of the University's Demonstration School. I was influenced by other mentors too, including Parent Counselor Corinne Sturtevant, M.S./ psychologist, Mary Leitch, J.D. /psychiatrist, I. H. Weiland, psychiatrist, and many others.

With the confidence of youth, I started my own Day Camp in 1951. I applied all that I had learned, and I continued to learn from the children. I became more and more aware of the necessity for reaching the whole child and all that was developing at this stage in their lives—physically, socially, emotionally, and academically—in other words, the "Total Child."

It was at this point that I started to formulate my dream: to provide a learning environment where the developmental needs of elementary-age children would be met through a more personalized approach to their style of learning and personality.

I started discussion groups with parents offering them a new way to participate in their children's social and emotional growth. I spoke about the importance of promoting their children's health in mind and body, a relatively new concept at the time. I also introduced a Global Learning aspect into the camp curriculum in order to foster learning about other cultures. We looked at similarities and differences around the world through play, song, dance, and drama.

Word spread, and, at the tender age of twenty-four, I was invited out to dinner with three sets of camp parents. They began the evening's discussion by letting me know how pleased they were with my approach, which they believed was directly tied to their children's progress, development, and well being. I was flattered, but did not see what was coming next. They proposed sponsoring me to create an elementary school of my very own where children could benefit from the "total child" philosophy all year round.

As soon as we parted company, my mind began to wander. The thoughts of making my dream a reality began to excite me more and more. I was fascinated by making a bigger difference in the lives of children and in partnering with parents to help them to understand and rear happy, productive children. But coupled with this elation was a real concern about my ability to bring all this to fruition.

Any doubts that I had were allayed by my professional mentors and those initial three sets of trusting parents. By inspiring my imagination, opening up my thoughts, providing me with new insights and ways of thinking, and guiding my vision for what was important in children's education, they made me feel that I could indeed make this happen.

My own parents were also incredible to me during this time. They had previously allowed me to operate my camp from their home, which sat on one acre of land in Valley Glen, California. After careful consideration, they agreed to let me use their property once again, but this time for my day school. So following conversations with many people, I decided that with the sponsorship of those three incredibly supportive couples, whom I can only describe as real-life guardian angels, I would move forward with the process of starting my own elementary school. My dream was actually beginning to become a reality.

This was really happening! On my parents' land and with the full approval of the LA City Department of

Building Safety and Health, we began building a modest two-room schoolhouse with restrooms. The three founding families covered the cost of construction and made tuition payments to me as well. Their generosity extended to assuring me that I wouldn't have to pay them back until I could. I couldn't have been more fortunate. The timing was right, they gave me the confidence to move forward, and they provided the costly resources as well. These incredible individuals will always hold a dear spot in my heart, and my gratitude knows no bounds.

It was in 1953 that Laurence School opened with a student body of thirteen. The children ranged in age from five to ten and we were a happy little family. Unlike my kindergarten teacher, I felt quite comfortable differentiating the instruction for this mixed age and ability group. I put into practice a "total child" approach and promoted core values such as cooperation, caring, respect for one another, and responsibility. We practiced these daily. I explained that we are a family—a school family where children could learn and be happy. I told these thirteen children that they were the most important people to me in the world and that each one of them had his/her own strengths, interests, and unique personalities, which I respected. I still tell my students this today. Together, those pioneers and I celebrated friendship, collaboration, and ability to interact together, and saw school as a place where we all could learn and have fun. But there was a very real difference between this family and their home family. At school there were very real expectations. Everyone knew that they had to listen, perform, support one another, and express their needs and wants positively. I believed then, as I do now, that effort and hard work make for happy and successful learners.

My work over the past six decades at Laurence School has been the true mission of my life. I am fortunate that from an early age I had a passion for learning which never wavered. I was lucky enough to turn this passion and dream into my life's work. It introduced me to wonderful children and parents and brought me satisfaction and excitement beyond anything I could have imagined. I am proud and grateful that this is my story.

Chapter One
About Laurence School

Good Morning, Good Morning!*
Good morning, good morning
I like the way you look!
Good morning, good morning to you

Good morning good morning
Say hi to your friend!
Good morning, good morning to you

Good morning, good morning
It is a wonderful day!
Good morning, good morning to you

**Sung to the tune of "Good Morning" (1939 song), sung by Nacio Herb Brown*
Used in the 1952 musical Singin' in the Rain

And so starts another traditional school-wide Friday assembly at Laurence School. These assemblies demonstrate on a weekly basis many of the core principles that go into making up a Laurence education: tradition, character development values (such as respect, kindness for others, honesty, responsibility, etc.), and the importance of every individual. In addition, they promote community service, and build self-esteem and leadership skills. Other opportunities are provided as well by student participation in our broad arts, drama, music and performing arts programs, and various sports activities. Combining all of those elements with our individualized approach to academic development and mastery are what make Laurence School what it is today.

Elementary education offers children the important start on the journey of their lives. I believe it is also the foundation for future learning and important for success later in life. After sixty years as founder of Laurence School, I still strongly believe in the "Total Child" philosophy for educating children. When asked why I continue to do what I do at Laurence School, I answer that it is because of the joy I experience in observing how children grow and thrive in our caring and loving environment every day. If you watch the children, you will understand my passion. I feel there is no place better for children to grow up, or for adults to be, than here at Laurence School. It truly is magic.

Academic Excellence

I would define academic excellence as a concentrated curriculum: breadth of subjects included with a few studies in-depth, high standards that challenge students, and a balance between academics and extra-curricular activities. It requires a different approach to teaching, one that encourages children not just to learn science or art, but to learn how to think like a scientist or an artist. It is important to recognize that every student comes from different circumstances and therefore has a different starting point.

People ask how to recognize academic excellence in a school. You need to spend a day at the school. You should see children who are serious about their purpose in being at school, children who are authentically engaged. There is fearlessness among the students and faculty who confront their weaknesses and figure out how to overcome them, engage in setting their own goals, and work together to create a community of learners.

Parents want academic excellence. According to our parents, academically excellent schools foster values such as compassion, diversity, and respect, as well as maintain an environment that permits each individual to achieve his/her full potential regardless of learning style and subject matter. For academically excellent schools, curriculum works in authentic ways with real content—it moves away from textbooks and pre-digested information and towards integrating learning across the disciplines.

Other expectations of an academically excellent school's effect on its students include the discipline to tackle and succeed at intellectual challenges, the ability to make the best use of one's talents and skills, the understanding that hard work and success are linked, the curiosity to consider learning fun, the persistence to overcome complexity and difficulty, the confidence to share knowledge with other people, the drive to always try hard and reach farther, and the self-awareness to find a balance between "I need to push harder" and "I'm doing just fine."

Academic excellence involves reaching beyond the classroom to an enriched program of music, art, computers, physical education, and performing arts—a time when children can discover their talents and interests. Through challenging and differential curriculum, highly qualified teachers prepare children to think critically and creatively and stimulate their need to reach higher and think independently.

Academic excellence is where students perform at high levels in all curricular areas, especially in higher-order thinking skills and the foundation subjects of reading, language arts, and math. It means that all students are accountable for learning and continually improving on their current level of achievement. It means that the achievement gap between the highest and lowest achieving students is continually narrowing.

You can measure a school's academic excellence by looking to students' lives in the years following graduation. You would want to see students who pursue their education after leaving. An academically excellent school produces socially responsible graduates with skills and the commitment to make the world a better place. Academic excellence provides children with concepts and learning skills that will live on and be useful no matter how things change. Academic excellence creates students who go on to be deep thinkers and problem solvers.

Three key components of academic excellence are: time, mastery learning/mastery teaching process, and instructional alignment.

Beyond the Basics – Importance of the Arts in School

A large body of research indicates that students who regularly participate in the arts enjoy greater academic achievement than their peers who do not.

We continually find that many children may excel in the arts before they make big strides in their academic skill development. We truly believe that the arts are a unique tool to stimulate and enrich learning. They not only encourage children's imagination and creativity, but they make lessons in other subjects (history, environmental studies, etc.) more memorable and profound.

Creative skills learned in the arts can help boost reading comprehension and vocabulary. Spatial reasoning skills, learned through music, have been shown to help students to better understand mathematical concepts. At Laurence School, we have found that participating in the school plays, art classes (during and after school), music programs and lessons, and school orchestra help make the school experience more enjoyable for almost every student. They can also lead to a lifelong appreciation of the arts, for which students may develop a passion that will sustain them into adulthood.

Building a Caring Community

Laurence School is a "caring community," which is to say that it is a place where everyone—students, staff, teachers, and administrators—treats everyone else with kindness and respect. To accomplish this, students must play an active role in shaping the culture and environment of the classroom, as well as of the school at large. Here are some ways that we make it happen:

- Class meetings are held in which students establish group goals, decide on rules of conduct, plan activities, and solve problems.
- Students collaborate on academic tasks by working in cooperative learning groups. They are given regular opportunities to plan and reflect on how well they work together.
- We have a "buddy program" where younger and older students get together to work one-on-one on academic tasks and other kinds of activities.
- Conflict resolution and other social skills are taught so that students become skilled at resolving conflicts fairly and peacefully.

These strategies help students learn to establish and maintain positive relationships with others. They also turn the school into a laboratory where students practice the kinds of roles and cope with the kinds of challenges they will face later in life.

Service Learning

Caring and Sharing Helping Others

To encourage the spirit of giving and sharing year round and not just on special holidays Laurence School initiated an ongoing program called "Sharing our Food." Students contribute canned food and other basic necessities to the North Hollywood interfaith food pantry which is sponsored by the San Fernando Valley Interfaith Council.

Falling to mind the well know expression, Fridays Child is loving and giving, each student drops off cans of food and other needed items at our gate each Friday morning. Students in the schools leadership program, Student Council are taken to experience the food distribution.

We know that the children derive many positive feelings in helping others. This is truly an experience in giving. This is an important aspect of Humanistic Education that Laurence School proudly fosters in the ongoing program of "Caring and Sharing."

Character Education

Laurence School is strongly committed to teaching values to children—respect, responsibility, empathy, kindness, and concern for others. These are important values for children of all ages to learn, honor, and incorporate into their own personality. These values help build self-confidence and set the tone for all interactions on campus. Our mission is to emphasize to our students the importance of being positive members of the community who take action to help others. We teach and model this behavior and expose children to hands-on, project-based learning and inquiry opportunities that connect to the curriculum in all subject areas.

At Laurence School, we value character education so highly that we consider it to be an aspect of our core curriculum—no different from reading or math—as opposed to being an enrichment area. We strongly believe that children need to develop caring and concern for others from the time that they are young, and this program enables them to reach out to those who may not have the same advantages that they have and to do their part, no matter how small, to make a difference.

It is not enough for our students to just raise money; thoughtful service meets a real community need and is developmentally appropriate. Projects with environmental themes, for example, are suitable for all ages. From recycling drives to beach cleanups to tree planting field trips, Laurence children are bettering the world with their own hands, and they feel connected to their learning because they can see how their actions are solving real problems, from landfill overcrowding to deforestation. Other projects may emanate from the children themselves, and these are even more powerful.

Students may hear about various natural disasters happening around the world, and they may wish to get involved. Our second graders rallied the school community to donate relief efforts in their sister country, Japan, after a massive earthquake struck there. They decided to do their part first by volunteering to complete chores around their own houses in exchange for donation money. The fact that they had been studying about this country all year long gave their chore-a-thon even more meaning. Although they couldn't fly to Japan to help with the clean-up efforts, they could make a difference, and this was certainly more powerful than simply asking their parents to open up their checkbooks.

Campus community-building activities, such as morning meetings, weekly assemblies, community service, and active communication with parents, help to model this behavior. They also involve a very clear way of dealing with students and their feelings. The emphasis is on acknowledgement of a student's emotions and listening carefully to him/her without judgment. Positive language and clear, respectful communication are the keystones. The method validates feelings while offering students a safe way to express the strongest of emotions. It also helps them decide on what they should do next. Our faculty supports this approach and works hard to make it part of the fabric of the school. The result is that at Laurence School our students feel secure, self-confident, and respected.

Respect is the way one talks to someone and

sometimes it is following the rules. It is not only in regard to people. Children also need to learn about respecting things and understand that being respectful is one of the ways they can acknowledge another person. Respect means treating people the way you want to be treated. Everyone should be treated with respect. They also need to understand that respect is one of life's important values now and when they grow up. Implicit in demonstrating respect is the understanding "I know what I need to do in this situation." It is truly a complicated concept. It is hard for many adults to practice respect for others—imagine how difficult it is for children to master.

As parents and teachers, we need to communicate to children our expectation of how we want them to act, i.e. greeting visitors courteously, using appropriate language to resolve conflicts, expression of feelings, etc. Helping students develop the self-discipline they need to follow procedures and rules is an education that continually fosters character development and our goal.

At school, we use the following to help students develop positive character traits:

- Cooperative Learning: learning how to work with others, teaching them how to think, helping them evaluate ideas and perspective (i.e. reflect and reason)
- Meaningful Literature: offering reading that is rich in human drama
- Community Service Opportunities: providing students with the opportunity to give to and work with community organizations
- Good modeling by adults

Character education is truly a process—a process that builds from year to year. When the school and home create a positive partnership in this regard, the result is happy children who know how to be caring, respectful, and responsible. Both school and home need to teach values everyday! The partnership produces children who trust, have empathy, show respect, and are responsible for others.

Good Character is:

What you feel in your heart	Knowing what is good
What you think in your head	Wanting what is good
What you do with your hands	Doing what is good

Core Beliefs

Mission Statement

Our mission is unique and well articulated
There are clear goals for student development
The school is committed to the development of the individual student's potential
The school is an inclusive environment
It enhances the development of social and emotional skills

Philosophy

It has a values-based philosophy
It delivers individualized and personalized attention to all children
It puts a concentrated effort on instilling pride, tradition, and spirit
It has clear behavioral expectations
It utilizes ongoing self-evaluation
It is committed to diversity—staff and students

Program

The curriculum is integrated and sequential
The school is committed to technological competence
It believes in innovation and introspection
It uses the community, enrichment, and service learning to enhance the program
Emphasis is placed upon engaging students in meaningful learning

Learning Environment

Facilities meet or exceed the needs of the program
The environment is nurturing and aesthetically beautiful
The school has appropriate and beyond parent participation
There is effective and regular communication

Purpose

To provide personalized education of unparalleled excellence
To care passionately about our children and to recognize, support, and value every child
To provide a safe and nurturing environment for learning where children can thrive, learn, and develop according to his/her own learning style and developmental readiness
To be concerned about building a vibrant educational community predicated on showing joy and respect for self, others, and the entire environment
To know our students as individuals and honor their academic, cultural, and social differences
To believe that the "Laurence way" provides the best foundation for children as they become productive world citizens
To instill within our students a lifelong love of learning and the confidence and courage to try new challenges
To teach our children to think critically and creatively, to express themselves clearly, and to act upon their convictions
To affirm that home and school are united in constant partnership
To understand that each child learns in his/her own way and that each has a limited amount of psychic energy to listen, pay attention, and stay engaged in learning.

Global Education

The "Global Garden" Educational Program, an innovative, caring expression of good will, seeks to form meaningful, ongoing connections between Laurence students and like-aged children from across the world. Through letters, emails, videos, and/or photos, they share their interests, traditions, and customs, and explore each other's history.

Our school-wide study of global education invokes curiosity and stimulation for students as they trace their roots to discover information about their own family heritage and traditions as far back as they can possibly go. Along with the value of communicating with older family members, this opportunity provides information that opens new vistas as children experience many similarities and differences with their sister countries. They rejoice in the wonderment of sameness and are excited to learn about the differences—all the while learning respect and acceptance. Ultimately, this leads to a deeper appreciation of the uniqueness of all cultures.

The Internet enables us to bring to life how people live, play, learn, and respect life all over the world. The countries that we have connected Laurence School children with are: China, England, Japan, Egypt, Israel, Africa, and various states around our own country. We were all treated to an unforgettable experience when the Qantas Children's Choir of Australia visited our school to lead an assembly and share their experiences with our students! In this way, our Global Garden—Appreciating Identity, Being Global, Celebrating Similarities and Differences—comes to life for parents, teachers, and children.

Every year at Open House, as a culminating activity, the school hosts a major "Global Garden Fair." It is a time to celebrate a year of learning, giving, and interacting with a global world. Parents play a significant part throughout the year, not only in sharing their culture with the school community, but through displays in the library, sharing regalia, and by bringing food for the children. The "Fair" enables an entire community to experience learning about the sister country of each class. Booths are decorated with posters, artwork, information, clothes, music, etc. The students act as guides, assisting others in learning about their country's booth and the students they were in contact with over the year. Here, education comes with fun, food, and enjoyment for all.

The World of the Future

Go Global, Go Green

We need to prepare our children to live and function in a world which will be different from our own. Our world is full of changes, new ideas and new technology. Our children need to be prepared to think critically and to solve challenging problems of a social and technological nature which may confront them in their future years, i.e., water, energy, space, transportation, food, agriculture, etc.

Laurence School embraces a school-wide integrated, innovative curriculum "Earth Day Every Day, Go Global, Go Green". This environmental "green" theme highlights one of the most significant global and local challenges, as we explore what students can do at home, at school, and in the community to help preserve our natural treasures for future generations.

The aim of this study and indeed the entire curriculum is to get our students involved in the process of learning, not just the memorization of facts. The curriculum is designed to give students direct experience in science (STEAM science, technology, engineering, art, math) and to stimulate their curiosity and imagination.

Giving back to the community and the natural environment is a priority at Laurence School as we strive to nurture students who are both responsible citizens and leaders.

Our whole hearted commitment to promoting and implementing environmentally friendly practices and programs include:

- Facility Improvements – New compact fluorescent lights, energy saving light bulbs, and environmentally friendly carpets have been installed
- Recycling and Zero Waste Lunch – We have expanded on the school's recycling and Zero Waste Lunch programs and try to only use compostable and recyclable paper goods on campus
- Gardening Program and our Farmers' Market – Our organic gardening program empowers students to plant, nurture and harvest a variety of products to be sold at a Farmers' Market in the Spring and we have included a butterfly garden for observing the life cycle
- Environmental Field trips – We provide outdoor education based field trips per grade level to Catalina Island, TreePeople, Astrocamp, the Santa Monica Mountains and other surrounding natural habitats around Los Angeles
- Electronic Communication – Encouraging electronic communication of school publications (i.e. Backpack News) and teacher forms and flash drives provided to faculty/staff have all reduced paper consumption
- Enrichment Programs – School programs promote Environmental Awareness on topics dealing with sustainability, environmental stewardship, and protection of natural resources
- Waste Reduction – Personal water bottles have replaced disposable ones; cloth napkins are provided

to students for lunches, and we use natural gas buses for field trips

- Family Involvement – Carpools, recycling and reinforcing green concepts at home all reinforce this important concept for the children.

When we are asked—Do American students measure up? We, at Laurence can reply that we start preparing our students at kindergarten to work up to their potential and to be prepared to live in a technological world as caring, concerned people.

Importance of Learning

One of the primary ego functions that sustains adaptation and provides a means of coping with stress and overcoming obstacles is the capacity for formal structured learning. Being able to read or to manipulate numbers, knowing how to absorb and integrate a body of facts (as in geography or history), the experience of testing the truth of a general statement against available evidence (as in any science, but also in the effort to describe what a poem is about) does more than provide tools for future learning or skills by means of which to earn a living.

The experience of learning, and the perception of the self as one who can learn, generates a sense of the self as an active being and a sense of the self as the carrier of power and competence. It also makes available a source of pleasure and satisfaction that is not directly dependent upon the quality of interpersonal relationships. Last but not least, each instance of successful learning makes life more intelligible. Words, concepts, metaphors, and physical phenomena that are bewildering, out of context, and hence alien, become components of a comprehensible and orderly environment in consequence of successful learning.

Children who have learned to learn stand a better chance of surviving even serious trauma and deprivation than do those who never succeeded in mastery on an intellectual level.

Clearly, the best state of affairs is a combination of supportive and constructive human relationships in the schoolroom and positive experiences in the act of learning, with scope for the encouragement of creative talents as well.

Laurence School Story

Laurence endeavors to develop the unique abilities and potential of each of its students in a diverse, inclusive and supportive learning community, where rich traditions and an innovative curriculum foster educational excellence and joy in learning, pride in oneself, integrity, mutual respect and a commitment to the "Total Child."It has a reputation of having a challenging academic program that prepares students for admission to the finest independent secondary schools in the community. Since its inception in 1953, the physical nature of the school has changed tremendously, but what has stayed the same is its success with children and their families. The "Total Child" approach to education has always been the hallmark philosophy of the school. That is to say that children are not one-dimensional but multi-faceted. Their development depends on their social, emotional, physical, and intellectual health. Success in one area is not the goal. All of these aspects are intertwined and require support to ensure the child functions as a whole.

Laurence's paramount goal is to provide a strong academic program that remains on the cutting edge of education and encourages children to enhance and broaden their critical and creative thinking. The rich, well-balanced curriculum motivates students to understand important concepts, refine higher level thinking skills, explore their special interests and talents, engage in real-world discovery, and connect learning to their everyday environment. In this spirit, Laurence School has a long-standing commitment to instill children with the foundation and inspiration to become lifelong learners.

At Laurence School, something new is happening each day, whether in the classroom, in after-school enrichment, outside on the playground, or in the lunch areas. I marvel at the creativity, high-level thinking, and love of learning that our children and teachers possess. This appreciation and thirst for knowledge is part of the school's magic.

Our commitment to excellence and to teaching all children to be responsible, caring, and contributing members of the community is ever present. Through service learning and environmental and multicultural education, our children learn that the earth is bigger than their immediate environment of home and school. They also learn through our global education program, which reinforces our commitment to diversity, to understand and appreciate cultures other than their own. It is where children are prepared to become engaged, ethically responsible citizens with the confidence, knowledge, and skills to become future leaders. Service learning is integrated into the curriculum for all grades to help instill lifelong values associated with service to others both locally and globally. Character education has been another deep interest here. By stressing caring, responsibility, kindness, and empathy for others, we strengthen children's social/emotional well-being, which helps them to make good decisions and achieve their goals.

Laurence School is truly an extraordinary place—unlike any other, I believe, for children to learn and grow in a safe, nurturing, and intimate environment where respect and kindness for each other, children, and adults is evidence in the total school. Throughout their years at Laurence School, students begin to explore life's most important questions. They continually discover that what they learn in school makes a difference in their lives, their community, and, ultimately, in the world around them.

I believe children learn best when there is a welcoming and active partnership between school and family. This partnership is pivotal to the school community and strengthens the foundation for learning. Together we model shared values of responsibility, respect, empathy, and kindness toward one another.

There have been many physical changes to the school over the years. It started in 1953 as a two-room school, with a swimming pool, arts and crafts center in a garage, a huge play area with walnut, orange, and lemon trees, and a wonderful tree house that serviced twelve children ages five to ten years old.

In the late 60s and early 70s I felt a need to evaluate the value of our educational programs and approaches to children. I researched and applied for educational grants that were rejected. I then turned to the mental health area and learned that there was money available but it was necessary to be affiliated with a mental health facility. Consequently, as a nonprofit, Laurence School became a member of the San Fernando Valley Mental Health Center. I applied for, and was awarded, grants for Early Childhood Innovative Programs. This was a bonanza that allowed me to broaden the scope of our current program to include identified gifted children, musically, artistically, as well as academically. This led to the decision to phase out some students whose learning and behavioral needs were not being met so that this new population could thrive at

Laurence. It also led the way to applying for a second grant for a diagnostic teaching center to offer our services to teachers and parents who wished to know more about their children's learning and behavior needs. It also included a yearly conference sponsored by Laurence in collaboration with UCLA and Cal State Northridge.

In the 80s, busing became an issue and parents who had not thought of private education began to consider a change. Laurence School began to burgeon with many new gifted students and others who needed a total approach to development to meet their needs. To differentiate this new focus from the previous one, the school's name was changed to Laurence 2000. (The name changed back to Laurence School at the beginning of the 2001–2002 school year.)

Starting in the late 80s, Laurence received recognition with membership in the Western Association of Schools and Colleges (WASC). This oversight body requires extensive criteria to be met, exhaustive self-reflection and reporting, and rigorous follow up. We are proud of the excellent commendations and accreditation we have received over the years. Laurence School is also a proud member of the California Association of Independent Schools (CAIS).

Today, Laurence School is a five-acre campus that houses sixteen major classrooms for over 300 students, small learning labs, a music room, art studio, library, science center, indoor gym and performing arts center, and a green sports court. The growth of the technology center continues to be the hub for the highest-level equipment that plugs into the worldwide network of learning, which supports relevancy and higher learning skills for all grades. It is a campus that bustles with the vitality and energy that all of our wonderful students bring to school with them each day.

As Founding Director, it has been an inspiration for me to continue to move forward alongside the school with a vision to provide the best education for elementary-aged children. These years are so critical, as they are the ones during which children begin their educational journey and cultivate their foundation—success in developing skills in reading, writing, math, and beyond, as well as developing the all-important lifelong love of learning. It is our personalized approach to learning the basic skills based upon each child's developmental, social/emotional growth and maturation that enables our children to reach their optimum in learning potential.

Laurence School is a most grounded, forward-looking, worldly, and service-oriented school. It is a magnet that draws children to want to learn and to participate in life. Throughout its sixty-year history, the school's administrative team has envisioned and translated ideas and ideals into reality. Our focus has been on combining theory with practice and on creating an inclusive community, an enriched curriculum, and a service-minded, environmentally-conscious student body. We're always looking for innovative ways to bring problem-solving and critical thinking into the classroom.

The idea of schooling as we currently know it will struggle to remain relevant in a networked world. However, I still believe that schools and teachers have a hugely important role to play in each child's learning. The relationships that children form with adults and the many enriched activities provided every day in school are vital in children's total development. I have always accepted change as moving forward and a great opportunity to learn and try new things. It is not a threat. It has been an exciting and stimulating journey for me and the school.

Laurence School Timeline

1951	Day camp opened with 100 children
1953	Laurence School opens with thirteen students in a one-building schoolhouse with orange orchards and neighborhood horse trails
1953–1958	"Total Child" concept and emphasis on hands-on learning introduced
1959–1963	Parent discussion groups are formed focusing on child development; second building and original offices are added
Early 60s–70s	School received grants for Innovative Early Childhood Programs
1968	The school is incorporated as a non-profit organization
1970	School is expanded to include a music room, three more classrooms, tech center, library, and health office
1975	Lynn Jacobson becomes Co-Director
	School's name changes to Laurence 2000 to reflect the school's new direction: innovative, forward-thinking, and tech-savvy
1978	School receives Los Angeles City Council Award
Late 80s	First WASC Accreditation
1985	Computers introduced into curriculum
1988	Laurie Wolke joins the Administrative Team
1990	Swimming pool is covered over and two more classrooms are created

1993	Science lab added and art studio is remodeled
1995	Media center is created; computer lab updated with Pentium processors
1997	Gary Stern joins the Administrative Team
1997–1998	Expansion project adds new administration building, new classrooms, conference and tutorial rooms, grassy play area, new kindergarten rooms with separate play area, monitored Internet access throughout media center
2001	Name changed back to Laurence School
2005	Expansion project triples campus size, adds tech center, new library, performing arts center, Field of Dreams and two more classrooms allowing for two classes per grade level
	Additional WASC Accreditation given
2006	Edible Garden is created and planted
2007	"Fulfilling the Dream" multi-year capital campaign project launched
2009	Laurence School goes green
	Staff increased to 60—includes classroom teachers, team teachers, teaching assistants, additional specialists in science, music, and drama. "Build A Greener Greater Laurence" capital campaign launched
2010	Laurie Wolke appointed Head of School; Mr. & Mrs. Jacobson continue as Founding Director and Educational Consultant, respectively
	Lightening Field (regulation size state of the art turf sports and activities field) is opened,

	Team Sports Program developed, Smart Boards installed in all classrooms, administrative structure expanded to include full-time Business and Operations Manager, Curriculum Coordinator, Director of Technology and Academic Services, Office Manager and Development Associate & Assistant, Information Technology Specialist, Business Office Assistant, Communications Coordinator, and two secretaries
2012	Arts & Enrichment Alcove added
2013	Laurence School celebrates its Sixtieth Anniversary
2015	Laurence School teaches over 300 students in sixteen classrooms on a five acre, beautifully landscaped campus where the "Total Child" concept continues to thrive

Partnership for Sixty Years

My life has been made more wonderful by being able to share it with Lynn Jacobson, and I truly believe that our partnership has also been an important ingredient in Laurence School's success. Being two highly motivated educators who specialize in child development, curriculum, and the Total Child approach to education, we have spent our lives building Laurence School into what it is today.

Over the years as we have worked independently and collaboratively. We have supported each other and believed in the importance of encouraging all children to learn and succeed. Together we worked to create "I can" feelings within each child so that they could develop a positive self-image and a strong desire to be motivated to try and work hard.

Both of us believe strongly in the importance of creativity and curiosity in the curriculum. At Laurence School, these are key elements of our program and have helped to create "lifelong learners" of countless children from all backgrounds.

We are so gratified by the evidence of alumni students who, as young adults, report that their elementary school education played a significant part in developing the character traits that remain within them into adulthood and which contributed to their current success in life.

It has been my pleasure to work with Lynn on a daily basis over the past sixty years. Our conversations, minds, and hearts are constantly consumed by thoughts of how to build a better educational environment for young children so that they are prepared for success in an ever-changing world.

My story, and that of Laurence School itself, is richer, more successful, and for me, personally, more satisfying, because of the partnership that we have been able to share.

"Total Child" Approach to Education

In my early years at UCLA, my graduate work involved the study of elementary age children. I immersed myself in research and looked to mentor and psychologist Erik Emerson for the most current thinking about the growth and development of children. I also spent hours observing children of all ages in the elementary school setting. I began to understand how children truly learn. I saw the importance of play, hands-on learning experiences, and how motivated the children were to participate in groups. What excited me the most about these observations was the realization of how important the social and emotional component was in the academic process. I discovered how important is was for children between the ages of five and twelve to feel safe in a secure environment, that it was vital that they had friends, and that freedom from anxiety was necessary for them to learn effectively.

This research, combined with my experience in day camps, where I listened to and observed the children in dramatic play, were the impetus for my thinking about the child in totality. This influenced the creation of the "Total Child" approach to education, a philosophy that I am pleased to say has worked for so many children over the past sixty years.

The "Total Child" approach to education looks at, and guides, the child's development in social, emotional, physical, and academic areas. I believe, and Laurence School has borne me out, that only by incorporating all these facets of the growing child can a successful foundation in learning be achieved—and not just achieved, but done so in a way that nurtures the child and fosters a positive sense of self, incorporates good values into their view of others, and produces a framework for thinking that will last their entire life.

I have dedicated my life's work to Laurence School and the "Total Child" philosophy, and I am so pleased that six decades after its inception this approach to education resonates even stronger in the twenty-first century. With the future in our children's hands, I believe that this philosophy of learning will provide them with the confidence and the tools needed to face the challenges that they will meet.

Chapter Two
Children

A child comes into the world full of wonder and potential. All are unique and all are special. Research indicates the importance of stimulating the child in the first ten months of their lives and that crucial learning comes in the first five years.

All children come to school with different interests, abilities, and motivations to explore and discover the world around them. When children come into kindergarten between the ages of five and six, they have only been briefly exposed to expressing their feelings, developing social skills and friendships, and all are at a different point in understanding numbers, letters, writing, science, art, and music.

During the elementary school years, children will discover their own strengths and passions, build their self-esteem, gain problem-solving skills, and hopefully develop a lifelong love of learning.

The following pages express the insights gained from my years of working with, and being inspired by, young children and what I believe to be true.

Basic Needs of Children

Survival

The most basic need is the physical need for food, shelter, safety, and security. At home and at school, this translates into physical comfort and a sense of order. Unless children feel safe and secure, they cannot experience learning, fun, and the full experiences of life.

Love and Belonging

Children, like all of us, are social creatures. There is a definite relationship between the quality of the relationships in our lives and our physical and mental well-being. As parents and teachers, we need to help children develop a sense of belonging and acceptance.

Personal Power

The need to achieve, to gain knowledge and skills, to receive recognition, and to gain personal power are tied together and vital in the life of the young child. We can help children gain this appropriate power by including them in regulating their behavior, which helps them function well within the family structure and at school.

Need to be Free

When children are included in the choices being offered, either for family cooperative events or an activity at school, this freedom to choose is important as they begin to highlight their strengths and abilities.

Need for Fun

The importance of this time cannot be overlooked either at home or at school. Time to enjoy just being with others or alone in the pursuit of those activities that bring pleasure, give children's minds a much-needed break and provide balance to their days and lives.

Building and Developing Trust

Connecting with children is the most important thing we need to do. Trust means caring and being concerned about all areas of their well-being. It means being consistent in discipline approaches. It means being firm and fair. It means recognizing the "Total Child" and his/her growth and development in all areas of learning: academic, social, emotional and physical. It means "active" listening and reaching out to children to encourage them to tell us about their needs. All children need to see that their parents and teachers value their effort, curiosity, and courage in taking risks. All of these help build trust and foster a caring relationship with children. It has always been my practice to remember each child by name. To an elementary age child, knowing his/her name is the basis for forming a relationship and building trust. Understanding and knowing the family, siblings, grandparents, and especially the child's interests can be a basis for a strong relationship at school.

Caring

When children feel genuinely cared for, they in turn learn to be caring of others. Caring, however, is not simply a warm, fuzzy feeling for others. On a deeper level, caring inspires children to strive to do their best on behalf of those who care for them, be it parents and/or teachers.

Caring needs to be modeled. Personal demonstrations of caring by adults more profoundly influence children than any particular curriculum or pedagogy. School and home are places where students are cared for and learn to care for others. Every child needs positive role models to develop a genuine concern for others, for the natural world and its creatures, and for preserving the human-made world.

To teach children to care, children must learn to care about themselves and understand what it means to have an admirable character before they can care for others.

Have an open and honest dialogue about caring. Children must be given daily input about the value of caring in school and at home. Risks no doubt come with the territory, as significantly adults teach children to care. In our Information Age, children are constantly bombarded with examples of politicians, entertainers, athletes, and businessmen who seem to escape the law and profit from their transgressions. Parents and teachers should allow their children to raise these issues, discuss their concerns, and then be prepared to offset them with equally poignant examples of honesty, compassion, moderation, and charity exhibited by the overwhelming majority of famous and ordinary people.

Emotional Intelligence

Emotional intelligence is the ability to read people as well as we read books. It is how well we manage ourselves and get along with others. It manages feelings so that they are expressed appropriately and effectively and enables people to work together smoothly toward a common goal. It enables one to acknowledge and learn from our own feelings. It helps us to understand ourselves more accurately.

Unlike IQ, which is the intellect untainted by education. Half of all emotional intelligence (or EQ) is acquired through modeling and guidance of parents and teachers. It begins with parents prior to children beginning elementary school and develops even more quickly once the child begins school. The emotional abilities children acquire later in life build upon the earliest years. The emotional centers of the brain continue to mature until age fourteen and are shaped by repeated experience.

Research has shown that EQ predicts success in adults twice as often as IQ and that IQ only contributes twenty percent to a child's future success. The ability of a four-year-old to control an impulse has been a predictor of increased scores on standardized tests such as the ISEE and SAT. Children who were able to delay gratification at age five had less adolescent problems than those who couldn't.

Life success depends on how good a citizen, friend, partner, and worker you are. It has been shown to be very dependent on the following five qualities of emotional intelligence:

- Self-awareness
- Managing emotions
- Self-motivation
- Impulse control
- People skills—empathy for others and handling relationships smoothly

Success in school is not predicted by how "smart" a child is or their ability to read. School success and happiness for school-age children depend considerably on the following emotional and social criteria:

- Being able to wait, follow directions and to turn to the teachers for help
- Knowing what kind of behavior is expected and how to control impulses to misbehave
- The ability to express needs while getting along with other children
- Being self-assured and interested

Emotional intelligence is a different way of being "smart." In school, it plays a big role in school performance:

- To pay attention
- To manage distress
- To control impulsiveness
- To get involved in class discussions
- To be motivated to learn

In his book, *Emotional Intelligence*, Dr. Daniel Goleman explains that whether or not children arrive at school with the ability to learn depends greatly on how much the important adults in their lives have given them these seven key ingredients:

- *Confidence* – a sense of control and mastery of one's body, behavior, and world; the child's sense that he is more likely than not to succeed at what he undertakes and that adults will be helpful
- *Curiosity* – the sense that finding out about things is positive and leads to pleasure
- *Intentionality* – the wish and capacity to have an impact and to act upon that with persistence. This is related to a sense of competence, of being effective
- *Self-Control* – the ability to modulate and control one's own actions in age-appropriate ways; a sense of inner control
- *Relatedness* – the ability to engage with others based on the sense of being understood by and understanding others.
- *Capacity to Communicate* – the wish and ability to verbally exchange ideas, feelings, and concepts with others. This is related to a sense of trust in others and pleasure in engaging with others, including adults
- *Cooperativeness* – the ability to balance one's own needs with those of others in group activities

Emotional intelligence must never be overlooked or dismissed by parents or educators. In our desire for academic excellence, cognitive accomplishments, and success in later life as reflected by a high paying job, we must not forget the importance of this crucial component of a child's ability to truly succeed.

How Children Learn

Long term research studies indicate four of the greatest predictors of eventual success at the university level are achieved through the stimulation of learning starting at the early elementary school levels, namely: <u>the quantity and quality of discussion in the child's classroom and home, the clarity of value systems, the level of peer group support, and the amount of independent reading.</u>

<u>Learning at School</u>

Inquisitiveness, or curiosity, is what drives children's learning. Inquisitiveness leads to new knowledge. Learning is more than just good teaching and schooling. The brain is a living, unique, ever-changing organism that grows and reshapes itself in response to challenges, with elements that wither if not used.

Learning needs to be active and thinking needs to be constantly encouraged through good "Habits of The Mind."

Learning Process in Children

In all cultures, in all ages, learning of one kind or another has been the prerequisite of survival. The term 'learning' has many meanings, but let us think of it in terms of a process whereby experiences lead to change. This is accomplished by using both physical and intellectual faculties. Learning involves both body and mind. Ideas originate in our minds and then they are applied by using bodily functions. To the normal child, learning is as instinctive as breathing, eating, and eliminating waste; all of which are essential to survival.

For all children, the learning process starts the moment the child is born. The first year of life is the foundation for the future. It is here that nurturing, protection, affection, and relationship formulation take place. This gives a clue to the emotional pattern of all that is to follow. In the second and third years of life, the child learns to control his body and movements. He/she begins to relate to objects other than his/her mother. He/she is developing into an individual—a total being who is learning to control mobility and body functions. During the fourth and fifth year, he/she is involved in greater socialization and self-mastery. He/she has begun to know who he/she is—a boy or girl in relation to himself, parents, and siblings. Thinking and imagination become more highly developed—and by the sixth year and thereafter, the child is learning to broaden and strengthen his/her personality. There then appears a surge of intellectual readiness and capability. The child is curious and ready to utilize personal psychic energy for intellectual functioning. It is from the understanding of these patterns of child development that the school builds a curriculum to satisfy the strivings and needs manifested by children.

In considering a child's readiness for academic learning, we need to explore several areas. We need to know about general intelligence, actual functioning, and potential functioning. We need to know something of his/her neurological organization. What is his/her ability to communicate, to conceptualize, and to perceive? Is language capacity intact? What about maturation and its role in his/her readiness for learning?

To children, going to school and learning can mean many things. Who hasn't heard a child reply "nothing" when asked what he/she has learned at school? In many instances this may be true (in relation to "book learning"). To many children, what they feel through their senses may be more important than what they learn from books. Knowing this, the perceptive and knowledgeable teacher is always ready to provide experiences that will strengthen the sensory perceptions. This teacher will let them experience balancing themselves on a walking board to help develop laterality and directionality in terms of their bodies; let them feel with their hands in making an adobe brick or pounding a nail in the construction of a boat; give them the experience of learning to feel through the rhythms of music. This teacher will have them write about things they have seen, tasted, or smelled, and have them participate in planning an activity or sharing a swing with a friend. By doing this, the teacher is helping the child to perceive their teachers, as well as related adults at school, as people they can engage with and learn from in a meaningful and successful way.

These are some of the many vistas open to the normal child through which curiosity can be awakened, motivation to learn created, and desire to master basic skills in number concepts, reading, writing, and language instilled.

In this way, education can become an active and systematic process of fostering the acquisition of knowledge, skills, and controls, as well as the more intangible relationships between the teacher and the child.

It is a special time, between the ages of six and twelve, when children are ready for learning. The boundless energy of children needs to be utilized in a constructive way. For all children, learning needs to be a warm, gratifying, and exciting experience.

Making Every Child Feel Special at Laurence

Every child is unique and special. Each has his/her own potential to learn, grow in body and mind, and eventually to make a contribution to family, school, and future work.

All children need and want to feel this importance and specialness. Some children are able to express this feeling easily to parents and teachers, while others may find it more difficult to let adults know how they feel and how important it is to receive reinforcement for who they are.

What makes every child special is his/her unique qualities, talents, and desires. At Laurence School, a child's efforts to do his/her best in all areas of development—social, emotional, academic, and physical—merit praise when truly earned and deserved. Receiving sincere praise is an important part of helping children to feel special, as well as successful. Words like "No one is like you in the whole world"; "You have your own interests, skills, and personality"; "You are a caring and kind person with many strengths to be proud of" are the spiritual nurturance that every child should feel from the significant adults in his/her life.

It has always been my practice to remember each child by name. I greet him/her by name and try to comment about one of their interests or family members.

This helps each child know that they are recognized at school for being unique and special.

Every Friday, at the school's Red, White, Blue, and Green Assembly, we honor the children who are having a birthday that week. Each child is called up for a Laurence birthday ribbon. Happy Birthday is sung in English and Spanish. It is a great thrill to hear 300 of your fellow students applauding and cheering for you. And the following words are directed to each child celebrating a birthday: "You are unique and special. Each one of you has your own talents and interests. Even though many other people were born on your birthday, you are special and most important to everyone at school and in your family."

Primary Age Children

When children enter kindergarten, the need to further develop self-control and attention is a goal for all. Learning requires focus, paying attention, and the ability to control the need for immediate gratification.

Listening to and following directions enable children to enjoy and benefit from all the enriched activities in addition to beginning to master skills in reading, math etc.

Emotionally and socially, all children need to learn right from wrong by their parents as they participate in group activities on the playground as well as in the classrooms. They want to be part of the group; therefore, friendships become important and learning how "to give and take" enhances the need to successfully participate with others and enjoy the satisfaction of camaraderie with friends.

The Ages Between Five and Seven

Earning the trust of and respect for parents plays a significant role in children's development. It is a time when admitting error, exploring decisions, understanding why our family does things in a certain way—perhaps differently from other families—and expecting trust and caring will continue to be instilled in children's character as they grow and develop over the years.

RESILIENCY IN CHILDREN

Resiliency is the ability to "bounce back," to recover from a change, illness, social rejection, academic difficulties, and misfortune. Everyone has the ability to become resilient, but some children have a more difficult time than others.

One of the ways to help build resiliency in children is to encourage them to talk, talk, talk about their feelings, fears, and thoughts, especially as they pertain to events that frighten them. Our job is to listen, listen, listen. Too often adults want to tell children how they should feel, instead of listening to how they really feel. It is also common to tell children that everything will be okay or to explain why things happen. Unfortunately this is not very productive in helping children to build resilience.

WAYS TO BUILD RESILIENCY IN CHILDREN:

- Encourage children to ask for help when they need it. This ability is the primary mark of a resilient person.
- Validate fears during a frightening or threatening experience.
- Acknowledge some of your own fears.
- Limit exposure to internet, media, newspapers, etc.
- Practice relaxation techniques like deep breathing, etc.
- Encourage physical activity to discharge pent up anxiety.
- Listen to, or create, calm music.
- Encourage older children to write about their fears and discuss with an adult.

- Demonstrate support and family/school bonding during a crisis.
- Encourage to talk to adults and peers about their fears.
- Find ways for children to take appropriate concrete action in response to a crisis.
- Talk about past challenges and successes to build the child's confidence and show that they can do it and that difficulties can improve.

Research shows that children who are resilient tend to be:

- *Socially Competent* – They have the ability to elicit positive responses from others and establish nourishing relationships with adults and peers.
- *Problem Solvers* – They envision themselves as being in control, as having the ability to plan, and as being resourceful enough to know when and how to seek help from others.
- *Autonomous* – They have a sense of their own ability, act independently, and exert some control over their environment.
- *Goal Oriented* – They are persistent and have aspirations and a sense of purpose.

Seven Resilient Traits:

1. INSIGHT – Making a habit of asking thoughtful questions and giving honest answers.
2. INDEPENDENCE – Establish social, emotional, and physical distance from difficult feelings—steering one's own course.

3. RELATIONSHIPS – Making satisfying ties to other people.
4. INITIATIVE – Pushing for mastery—taking pleasure in solving problems.
5. CREATIVITY – Representing one's inner self in art forms.
6. HUMOR – Having the capacity to laugh at one's self and troubles.
7. MORALITY –Acting on an informed conscience.

Rewards of Hard Work

The best prize life offers is the chance to work hard at work worth doing.
–Theodore Roosevelt

Motivation is fantastic and goals are great, but nothing happens until hard work is added. If something is worth achieving, it's worth an all-out effort. The good things in life come to us as the result of time, energy, sacrifice, and even the risk of failure. So success requires a certain amount of toughness. It comes to people who aren't afraid of a challenge and some good old-fashioned hard work. If we want our dreams to come true, hard work has to be part of the formula.

But the best thing about hard work is that it does more than make our dreams come true. It has other rewards and benefits. Here are ten of them:

1. *Hard work helps us realize our potential.* As our work begins to pay off, it stimulates us to increase our effort. It helps us see what's possible. Success brings confidence, and confidence brings more success.
2. *Hard work helps us face up to life.* Life is hard. We're challenged every day to choose between whimpering about it or standing up to it. Hard work and a good attitude are the best tools we have.
3. *Hard work makes us feel good.* There's no greater feeling of satisfaction than in completing a task and knowing that we've done our best.

4. *Hard work builds character.* There's no better measure of who we are than our willingness to work. Enduring and honest effort brings out the best in us.
5. *Hard work earns the respect of others.* We're admired when we give our best, especially when it's done consistently. We earn the confidence and trust of others. We also earn a solid reputation.
6. *Hard work earns self-respect.* Consistently giving our best also helps us develop respect for ourselves. Whether we succeed or not, we always feel better when we try.
7. *Hard work adds meaning.* Working toward our goals is one of the most meaningful and rewarding experiences in life. As long as we have a purpose, we have a good reason to get out of bed in the morning.
8. *Hard work gets the best results.* Life is more interesting and enjoyable when we're productive. Fulfillment is the result of wholehearted effort.
9. *Hard work becomes a habit.* Habits are the key to all success, and the best three are honesty, politeness, and hard work.
10. *Hard work is healthy.* When we work hard, we use the mind and body in a positive way, so it induces both mental and physical health. Hard workers are healthier and live longer. Hard work is good for us.

Rights And Responsibilities Of Children

Children have the right to their feelings...

And have the responsibility to move beyond their feelings to action and caring about the feelings of others.

Children have the right to their own opinions...

And have the responsibility to listen to the opinions of others.

Children have the right to have fun...

And the responsibility not to disturb others while having fun.

Children have the right to be unique...

And the responsibility to respect others even though they're different.

Children have the right to be competitive and to win...

And the responsibility to be a good sport when they don't win.

Children have the right to make mistakes...

And the responsibility to learn from their mistakes and to correct them.

Children have the right to play and use the common living areas...

And the responsibility to clean up after themselves in rooms and spaces that everyone uses.

Children have the right to learn...

And the responsibility not to interfere with other's rights to learn.

Children have the right to have friends...

And the responsibility to present themselves as friendly.

Children have a right to make their own decisions...

And the responsibility to accept the consequences, good or bad.

Children have the right to their own attitude...

And the responsibility to expect what their actions produce.

Formal education can play a large part in helping children develop a healthy and good self concept. The attention (focus) and concentration (staying with the task) required in the classroom, as well as the ability to give and take with peers on a regular basis, are positive contributing factors in building a child's self concept.

Self Concept

What We Want Children to Perceive About Themselves

Goals: The Significant Seven

1. The child needs to believe he/she is a capable person and can solve problems if he/she tries.
2. He/she needs to believe he/she can contribute to a relationship with others that is important to him/her through his/her creativity, ideas, and resourcefulness.
3. He/she needs to believe he/she can find a way to alter circumstances or his/her responses to them in order to influence his/her environment.
4. He/she needs to show some ability for self assessment, self control, and self discipline.
5. He/she needs to show ability to communicate, cooperate, negotiate, share, empathize, and listen.
6. He/she needs to show some understanding of limits and consequences, privileges and responsibilities, cause and effect and his/her role in dealing with them.
7. He/she needs to have the ability to apply abstract notions—such as can/can't afford—in coming up with solutions and practical problems.

Stress in Children

Stress is an inevitable part of each of our lives. We can't always avoid it, but we can certainly learn to manage it. According to a stress survey published by the American Psychological Association, "Most Americans are suffering from moderate to high stress, with 44% reporting that their stress levels have increased over the past five years." Not surprisingly, money, work, and the economy were the top reported stressors, with job stability being another major source of stress (close to 50% of those surveyed stated that is caused them undue concern).

But, it's not just we adults who are experiencing stress—kids are feeling its effects too. Close to one in three children say that they've felt the physical symptoms of stress in the last month, including: headaches, stomachaches, vomiting, bed-wetting, irritability, crying, hair loss, nervous ticks, angry outbursts, or withdrawn or bullying behaviors. So, while parents may believe that their children are safe from the insidious world of stress, their children would beg to differ.

In a classroom, a stressed child may look distracted. He/she might have trouble concentrating or following directions, or perhaps she/he teases her/his classmates excessively. Underneath this stressed young person is a stressed body, and we (adults) must do our best to alleviate the tension.

It is widely reported that the serotonin released during exercise is an effective stress-reducer. Promoting physical activity among students can be an important outlet for their stress too. It is important to provide children with ample opportunities to get out on the courts and fields, during and after school. Encouraging children to participate in an enjoyable extracurricular activity of some kind can be another effective way to lessen stress.

What teachers can do to help children cope with stress:

- Instruct students to take three deep breaths when anxiety begins to creep up on them.
- Have students write their feelings down in a journal.
- Suggest that students do something expressive and artistic (drawing, painting, pottery).
- Be an active listener to students (the most important tool of all) so that they will feel comfortable talking to teachers and administrators about their stresses and symptoms.

What parents can do to help children cope with stress:

- Acknowledge your child's feelings.
- Develop trust with your child and let him/her know that mistakes are learning experiences.
- Be supportive and praise your child for efforts he/she makes to communicate with you.
- Share and care (warmth and love); hug your child often.
- Have clear expectations without being too rigid.
- Keep your child's schedule manageable (do not sign him/her up for too many activities).
- Find ways to have your child contribute to the family.
- Build on your family's strengths.

- Be aware of what your child needs and wants, rather than what you need and want for him/her.
- Help your child to develop coping skills needed for future success.
- Set a good example for your child by keeping calm and controlling your own anger.
- Share new stress management ideas with your child.
- LAUGH—this is the best medicine of all!

Find the humor in life so your child will adopt the same mentality, incorporating your strategies into his/her stress toolbox. Share the laughter.

TEMPERAMENT

Temperament is a person's characteristics or traits that are biologically based and consistent over time. It is important for parents and teachers to discover a child's temperament and to help them understand how to work successfully within these traits. These usually cannot be changed, but accommodations can be made so that no matter what a child's temperament they can be successful at home, at school, and in life.

Basic Temperament Traits include:

Activity Level
Biological Rhythm
Approach and/or Withdrawal
Responsiveness
Intensity of Reaction
Quality of Mood
Distractibility—Attention Span and Persistence
Sensitivity—to sounds especially

What All Children Need to Know

- You are one of a kind.
- You have your own talents, strengths, and weaknesses.
- You can learn even if it takes you longer to master a skill. Making mistakes is part of all learning. We learn from our mistakes.
- You need encouragement and support to reach your potential—use the help of teachers, parents, and friends.
- You need to try to do many things to develop what you like and know what you can be good at.
- You need to know and believe that "I can." Trying is your best friend. It will bring you the results you need to make you feel good.
- Understand that anxiety and fear of failure are part of all new learning for everyone.
- Once you find something that really interests you, pursue it, and understand that to becoming proficient at it will require practice and hard work.

School-wide Symbols, Drawings, and Poems

CHAPTER THREE
Parenting the "Total Child"

THOUGHTS FROM A PARENT

Our children sleepily walk from their personal world through the gates of Laurence School each morning, and suddenly their day is awake and colorful with the bloom of life and learning.

They have entered a Secret Garden.

Lovingly fed a broad mixture of academics, music, art, socialization and much much more, they have blossomed.

Along with their peers, our children have grown into young people with a thirst for knowledge, a zest for improving our world of tomorrow and an appreciation of living in today's society.

Thanks for planting and continually nurturing the Secret Garden that is Laurence School.

Patti Claybourne

My years of working with children have given me a unique perspective and numerous insights that have educated me beyond my own experience as a parent, teacher, or my years of study in the field. I hope the words in this section will be useful as you nurture and support your child during their early school years.

The school and the teachers cannot do it alone. The part you play as a parent cannot be minimized. The partnership created between school and home is vital in helping your child to reach his/her full potential. In addition, it makes these formative years of exploration and growth exciting and satisfying for your family as well.

Parenting is an extraordinary act that takes extraordinary people to do it well. It also takes thoughtful reflection and continual effort to be the kind of parent a child respects and loves and who makes a difference in his/her life.

It is important for you to believe in yourselves and in your parenting as well as what you feel you want your children to feel you mean to them. Connecting and communicating with your children is the most important thing that each parent needs to do.

Your lives as parents of young children are busy and stressful, but hopefully the insights in this next section offer you a way to make the time you spend with your child more meaningful, enjoyable, and satisfying for all.

Attachment and Relationships

Throughout life, each of us will form thousands of relationships. These bonds take many forms. Some are enduring and intimate, our dearest friend; while others are transient and superficial—the chatty store clerk. Together, relationships in all forms create the glue of a family, community, and society. This capacity to form and maintain relationships is the most important trait of humankind, for without it none of us would survive, learn, work, or procreate.

The first and most important of all relationships are "attachment bonds." Initially, these are created through interactions with our primary caregivers, usually parents. First relationships help define our capacity for attachment and set the tone for all of our future relationships.

What is Attachment?

Attachment is the capacity to form and maintain healthy emotional relationships. The capacity to create these special relationships begins in early childhood. An "attachment bond" has unique properties. The unique features of an "attachment bond" are:

- Enduring bond with a special person
- Involves soothing, comfort, and pleasure
- Loss, or threat of loss, of the special person evokes intense distress
- There is security and safety in the context of this relationship

At birth, a baby is essentially emotionally "unattached." Despite the obvious physical connection of the umbilical cord, the newborn does not yet have strong connections to another human. During infancy and early childhood, one form of attachment—social-emotional—begins to replace the original physical attachment of the cord. As dependent as ever, a baby requires constant attention and care from another human being in order to survive. Calories and a "bath" of physical sensations—sight, sounds, smells, touch, and taste—help the infant survive and grow to meet his/her potential. This "somatosensory" bath from a loving caregiver—the rocking, hugs, coos, and smiles—is transformed by the infant's sensory systems into patterned neuronal activity that influences the development of the brain in positive ways. It is within this dependent relationship between the primary caregiver and the infant that a new form of attachment grows. This attachment—the emotional relationship—is not as easy to see or document, yet it is nonetheless as important for human development as the umbilical cord is *in utero*.

It is these experiences of infancy and early childhood that create the roots of attachment—the capacity to form and maintain healthy emotional relationships. Except in the most extreme cases, we are all born with the genetic capacity to form and maintain healthy emotional relationships. When the infant has attentive, responsive, and loving caregiving, this genetic potential is expressed. And as this infant becomes a toddler and more people—family, friends, peers—enter his/her life, he/she will continue to develop this capacity to have healthy emotional relationships.

Attachment and Pleasure

Our brain is designed to promote relationships. Specific parts of the human brain respond to emotional cues (such as facial expressions, touch, scent) and, more importantly, allow us to get pleasure from positive human interactions. The systems in the brain that mediate pleasure appear to be closely connected to the systems that mediate emotional relationships. Indeed this inter-relationship—the capacity to get pleasure from other people—creates a major positive learning tool of infancy and childhood. Young children want to please their teachers. They model themselves after adults and other children they admire.

When attachment capacity develops normally, the child gets pleasure from interacting with other people. The degree of pleasure is related to the degree of attachment—pleasing a parent brings more pleasure than pleasing a stranger. It is this very property that helps parents and teachers shape pro-social behaviors in a child. In the process of teaching children emotional, social, and cognitive tasks, the strongest rewards for a child that the parent or teacher can give are attention, approval, and recognition of success. Conversely, when a child feels he has displeased a parent or teacher, he can be devastated.

Attachment Capacity Matures

In order to be capable of forming the wide array of healthy relationships required throughout life, a young child's attachment capacities must mature. While the roots of attachment are related to the primary caregiving experiences in early childhood, full expression of attachment potential requires social and emotional interactions with non-caregivers. As children become older, they spend less time with parents and more time with peers and other adults providing many opportunities for continued emotional growth. In early childhood, the relationships with peers start as acquaintanceships. With more time together, however, young children create friendships and the opportunity for strong emotional bonds can develop. In a similar fashion, a young child may form a strong connection with an attentive and nurturing teacher. The acquaintance, the friend, and the teacher will provide different social and emotional opportunities that help a child's attachment capabilities mature.

When Attachment Goes Wrong

If a child has few positive relationships in early childhood or has had a bad start due to problems with the primary-caregiving experiences of infancy, that child is at risk for a host of problems. In a very real sense, the glue of normal human interactions is gone. A child with poor attachment capacity is much harder to "shape" and teach. This child will feel little pleasure from the teacher's smile or approving words. And he/she does not feel bad disappointing, angering, or upsetting a parent or teacher.

Without the capacity to use human interactions to "reward" and "punish," the teacher and parent often are confused and frustrated in their attempts to promote appropriate social behavior. In extreme cases, a child with poor attachment capacity demonstrates no remorse when harming others and risks developing further anti-social or even aggressive and violent behaviors. This child needs help. Research shows that attachment capacity is easiest to shape if early identification and intervention takes place.

What you can do to promote the development of healthy attachment:

- Smile and look your child in the eyes as you talk with him/her.
- Spend one on one time with your child. Quantity matters.
- During this time, listen and establish eye contact.
- Use touch to comfort—it is appropriate to hug, gently touch a shoulder, or hold hands.
- Help children learn appropriate social-emotional language (how close to stand, space issues, how to use eye contact, when to touch, how to touch).
- Remember that there are many styles of forming and maintaining relationships—a shy child is not an unattached child. If a child is having a hard time engaging others, help facilitate this by actively seeking out another child who has a matching temperament.

Character Education at Home

The development of good character is a lifelong endeavor, beginning in early childhood and continuing throughout the years. This is what develops a "conscience" that will guide them when parents are not around. By having your child understand what good character is at an early age, it will shape their minds and form their thinking in ways that are beneficial to themselves, their family, friends, community members, and other citizens in a global society.

Research indicates that the most important influence on children's character is the values the parents embody and model in the presence of their children.

Values are internalized by children not so much through instruction as through watching their parents' ways of thinking and being. "We teach who we are" whether we are aware of it or not. This is a most exacting, humbling, and rewarding task.

Model at home, at restaurants, and in all interactions the important values of kindness, caring, good manners, courtesy, politeness, and respect. By doing this your children's interpersonal behavior will be positive and satisfying as they see the good feelings of all involved that are generated by their actions.

Positive character traits, such as responsibility, perseverance, self-discipline, compassion, honesty, courage, fairness, respect, and integrity, give your children the confidence to participate and be influential in affecting change in the world. These values promote socially beneficial ideas, decision-making, and action when it comes to respecting the rights of others, protecting the environment, and putting an end to problems that exist worldwide.

Parents can reinforce these values, in addition to modeling, through good literature, surrounding the child with other good models, with family rules, by talking to your child, and having no tolerance for behavior that runs contrary to these values.

Here are some practical tips:

- Work to create a home environment that recognizes the destructive effects of put-downs (teasing, saying unkind things to others, making people feel sad or unhappy) and reject their use in all interpersonal interactions.
- Reinforce your children for using polite language, i.e. "thank you," "please," "excuse me," saying "Good Morning," "How are you today?" etc.
- Let your children know that it is not respectful to interrupt someone who is talking.
- Teach your children the importance of following the rules, starting with your family rules.
- Reinforce your children very positively for listening the first time when asked to do something.
- Virtues develop through practice. Give your children appropriate tasks or chores (without pay) to help them develop a sense of responsibility and caring within the family.

- Tell your children where you, as parents, stand on important matters, (e.g. war, peace, the environment, helping the poor, money, friends, school achievement, in appropriate language, trying for best effort, etc.)
- Manage the Moral Environment – regulate the use of media as a privilege and not a right. Know when parent presence is necessary. Let children know what is noble and heroic in the media.
- Have and enjoy family meals together (with no TV or other technological devices) as often as possible; the more the better.
- Plan as many activities as possible, involving children in the planning.
- Encourage and provide choices to develop independence.
- Explain why it is wrong to lie and cheat.
- Solve conflicts fairly by advancing a mutual understanding, arriving at a fair and agreed upon solution, and following up to evaluate how the solution worked.
- Reinforce the importance of giving eye contact when speaking to someone.
- Model all of the above, which works much better than lecturing.

Chores

Parents today want their children spending time on things that can bring them success, but, ironically, we've stopped doing the one thing that's actually been a proven predictor of success—and that's household chores. Decades of studies show the benefits of chores—academically, emotionally, and even professionally.

Giving children household chores at an early age helps to build a lasting sense of mastery, responsibility, and self-reliance, according to research.

Young adults who began chores at ages three and four were more likely to have good relationships with family and friends, to achieve academic and early career success, and be self-sufficient, as compared with those who didn't have chores or who started them as teens.

Chores also teach children how to be empathetic and responsive to others' needs.

Personal happiness comes from strong relationships. A good way to start readjusting priorities is by learning to be kind and helpful at home.

Here are some of the best ways to get your children properly motivated to do chores:

- *Schedule Chore Time.* Write chores into the calendar, right next to the piano lesson and soccer practice, to maintain consistency.

- *Game it.* Like a videogame, start small and have young children earn new "levels" of responsibilities, like going from sorting clothes to earning the right to use the washing machine.
- *Keep allowances and chores separate.* Research suggests that external rewards can actually lower intrinsic motivation and performance. With chores, psychologists say that money can lessen a child's motivation to help, turning an altruistic act into a business transaction.
- *Types of task matter.* To build pro-social behavior like empathy, chores should be routine and focused on taking care of the family (like dusting the living room or doing everyone's laundry), not self-care (tidying one's bedroom or doing personal laundry). Psychologists stress that involving children in choosing the tasks makes them more likely to buy in.
- *Talk about chores differently.* "Let's do our chores." This underscores that chores are not just a duty but also a way of taking care of each other.
- *Give chores a PR boost.* Don't tie chores to punishments. Keep any talk about chores, including your own, positive or at least neutral. If you complain about doing the dishes, so will your children.

Commitment to School and Learning

Making School the Top Priority for Children

In their desire to provide the very best for their children, parents often provide numerous extracurricular activities for their children throughout the school year. During summer vacation, children should rightfully participate in day camp, resident camp, and enrichment activities in the community as well as the all-important family vacation. During other school breaks, the same is true.

Children start school energized after as much as a month or more away from school, whether it be at day camps, overnight camps, sports camps, music and drama camps, traveling, or relaxing at home. These important experiences all come under the heading of "fun recreation" and are appropriate for vacations from school.

Once school resumes though, the goal is to prepare for new learning that contributes to each child's total development. At this time, school should have top priority in every student's life. Other enrichment activities should be of secondary importance.

Learning in all areas, especially a more structured routine, requires a different kind of energy—listening, paying attention, focusing, and an openness for motivation with a variety of new experiences to stimulate the mind and heart. To be successful learners, children need to devote a great deal of attention, focus, and energy to schoolwork, homework, and developing and maintaining positive peer relations.

Learning cannot always be fun or based upon personal interest. Each class has its own program that sparkles with fun and high interest activities that have appeal for every student. Because we all live in a visual world, education needs to breathe excitement into the mundane. Therefore, all students need energy for learning that will lead to optimum achievement and self-esteem based upon their developmental age and grade. A highly enriched curriculum with creative and motivating activities at each grade level requires total immersion of each child's psychic energy.

The goal is to motivate every student to be available to new learning and challenges and become excited about the wonders of life. The mastery of skills has a definite effect upon self-esteem. There is evidence that children who learn how to learn in the elementary years have a far better chance for success as they enter secondary school, adulthood life, and the workforce.

In order for teachers to do an excellent job of teaching, the attention and availability of their students is the most important. Outside activities should be kept at a minimum to keep school and learning as the top priority.

In a positive parent-school relationship, parents are encouraged to focus their child's total energy on school rather than auxiliary activities offered after school and on weekends. The most important question to ask is "What activities should take precedent in my child's life?" School and learning should rank at the top of the list. Nothing will better equip children for future success than devoting their wholehearted attention and energy to the plethora of enriched learning experiences at school. Equally important, children need to spend time after school and on weekends relaxing, thinking, reading, and recouping energy consumed during their seven to eight hours of active involvement at school.

Conception Story

I/We have been waiting for you to be grown up enough to ask about how a baby gets to grow in his/her mother. You are now old enough to ask me/us these questions. I/We are so proud of you and your curious mind that wants to find out about how you and others started. Usually, boys and girls of your age begin to think about this important question.

I/We want to tell you how you first started to grow inside your mother's womb. It takes a Daddy and a Mommy to start a baby. You see, there's a tiny cell inside the Mommy, and there's another very, very small cell inside the Daddy (Draw two dots a few inches apart.) The Daddy cell is inside his testicle. That's a little sac-like place that attaches to the body right next to the penis. Now the Daddy cell has to get together with the Mommy cell before the baby can start to grow. So, when the Daddy and the Mommy are feeling close and very loving to each other, the daddy moves his penis into the vagina passageway. That is called the birth canal. And while his penis is in there, he lets his little cell go out in about a tablespoon of liquid (fluid). And then, after he has moved his penis away, his little cell joins with the Mommy cell and the baby starts to grow.

So it takes a Daddy and a Mommy to start a baby. Now what else would you like to ask me/us that will help you understand the wonderful story about how you came to be ______________________(child's name)?

Cooperation Between Parent and Child

An attitude of understanding and acceptance will bring peace. Parenting skills to increase cooperation will help you and your children feel successful. The foundation for all of these skills is kindness and firmness at the same time: kindness to show respect for the child, and firmness to show respect for what needs to be done.

All of the positive discipline books are filled with parenting skills that are non-punitive and non-permissive (kind and firm) and which encourage positive long-range results, such as important life skills for success (becoming happy, contributing members of society) and perceptions of courage, confidence, and competence (developing healthy self-esteem).

Following are twelve of the many parenting skills that greatly increase cooperation. The first six are centered on motivating children; the last six focus on what you can do that doesn't depend on the child's cooperation (yet may increase cooperation in the long run).

- Involve children in pre-planning. Children are more likely to follow a plan that they have helped create.
- Take time for training to be sure your children know how to accomplish a task.

- Get children involved in creating a bedtime routine chart and a morning routine chart. Of course, part of the bedtime routine should be for children to choose and lay out the clothes they want to wear in the morning. These should be fun routine charts including pictures cut out of magazines or drawn for each task and posted in a conspicuous place.
- Let the routine chart be the boss. Ask, "What is next on our routine chart?" Children are much more responsive to this than to demands or lectures about what they should be doing.
- Hold regular family meetings so children can learn appreciation attitudes and skills, communication skills, and problem-solving skills. When things don't work, put the problem on the agenda and let the children figure out a solution—over and over and over.
- Ask what and how questions: "What are you supposed to be doing now?" (This is much different than telling a child what she should be doing.) "What was our agreement?" "How could we solve the problem we are now having?" "I really need your help. What would you be willing to do?" (When asked in a friendly tone of voice, these questions usually invite children to use their power to cooperate instead of to resist.)
- Remember that less is more. The less you say the more children will listen. Try one word, "toys," or less than ten words ("I would appreciate your help"), or no words: smile and point at what needs to be done.
- Take a shower so you aren't tempted to interfere, and so you don't invite a power struggle. Have faith in your child to do what is needed.

- Close your mouth and act. Instead of repeating a request over and over, take your child by the hand and lead him to what he/she needs to be doing.
- Use reflective listening to validate a child's feelings about how difficult it is to do what she/he doesn't want to do (while firmly leading her/him to what needs to be done).
- If you say it, mean it, and if you mean it, follow through. (If you say you won't drive while children are fighting in the car, pull over and read a magazine the minute they start fighting. If you don't say a word, they will soon stop. Words invite excuses and arguments.)
- Last but not least, put the relationship first. Make sure the message of love gets through. Understand mistaken goal behavior and deal with the belief behind the behavior. Help your child develop perceptions of belonging and significance.

Many parents think these suggestions are too time consuming. Yes, children are time consuming. And these skills are actually less time consuming than lectures, scolding, and all forms of punishment that only increase resistance. When parents remember and accept the reasons why children don't always do what they know they are supposed to do, they can exchange frustration for the fun of using effective parenting skills.

Coping with Loss

Grief is a normal human reaction to loss and is an emotion everyone experiences, even young children. In the past, it was thought that the best way to help children cope with loss was to essentially pretend that nothing had happened. Today, however, most experts agree that children and adults heal best if they are allowed to grieve, and are then given support and comfort to overcome the loss. Here are some ways you can help your children cope with grief:

Involve the school. Tell your child's teacher if grief has touched your child's life. Most teachers are familiar with helping children deal with short-lived loss, such as the death of a pet or a best friend moving away. Talk to both the teacher and the school administrator if a more significant loss has occurred, such as divorce or death. These people are skilled at helping children heal, making sure the child has time alone if necessary, ensuring that extra homework help is available, and helping classmates provide the right kind of support. Consider asking the school or local librarian for books about children coping with grief.

Watch behavior. Children may or may not display different behaviors in response to a death or other life-changing situation. Signs to look for include detachment, hyperactivity, anger, and lack of emotion. Some children may regress and want to be rocked or to sleep in their parents' bed. In addition, children may repeatedly ask questions because they are having difficulty believing or accepting the loss.

Give them a journal. Encourage elementary school-age children to write down their feelings—both good and bad—in a special notebook. Reassure them that it's fine to express anger or sadness, and it's equally all right to write down funny memories or anything else that may be on their minds. Keep it relaxed, so that the writing is viewed as a "release" and not homework.

Try art therapy. Provide art materials—paints, modeling clay, paper, crayons, colored pencils, or scrapbook kits—and encourage art therapy. Talking about the art they create can be an excellent way to keep communication lines open during tough times.

Be honest. Answer children's questions with age-appropriate information. In the case of a death, make sure your children know it's acceptable to talk about the person over whom they are grieving. Regardless of the type of loss, it's important that your children are able to keep their feelings and memories alive.

Talk about it. While it's very important to allow your children to talk about their feelings, don't pressure them into discussing things before they're ready.

Stick to a routine. Try to get back to your regular schedule as soon as possible. During the grieving process, see to it that children get regular exercise and enough sleep. And don't let children miss too much school.

Give them time. Grief is incredibly difficult for everyone. Children need long-lasting support, as it may take a long time for them to understand their feelings. School administrators and teachers can be a great first resource for parents looking to help their children cope with grief. They also can provide referrals to other counselors, both for the child and the family, if needed.

Above all, remember that your children hurt, just as you do, when grief strikes your family. Let them cry when they need to, laugh when they feel like it, be alone when they must, and be with you as much as they can.

Delaying Gratification

Research has shown that the ability to delay gratification in childhood is an indicator of success in later life. Delaying gratification at appropriate levels builds self-control.

When parents give in to a crying toddler/ preschooler, they do not teach their children self-control. Practice is vital in delaying gratification. Parents should not respond to your children's every whim or plea. Let him/ her deal with frustration and with hearing "no" that could have a growth element to it. Children need to learn to self-soothe when they can't have what they want and to accept that, at this time, it is a "no." They will learn to adjust when they don't get what they want and will come to discover that things will be all right, even when they have to wait. They will also learn to accept that life doesn't always grant us a "yes."

With delayed gratification, pre-teens are better equipped to handle the environment in middle school and beyond when drugs and alcohol become prevalent. Building foundations of self-control are hard to start in the pre-teen and teenage years, so it is better to start them early on.

Children need to learn at a young age about the things that can have a positive influence in their lives. A good example of this is the importance of having friends who share similar goals and values and with whom they can relax and be themselves. How to be able to stand up and say "no" when it is warranted is another vital skill, especially in respect to privacy.

Parents need to understand that success is not always possible in their child's learning. Weaknesses can be opportunities to learn about the value of practice and hard work. Failure can also open wide doors. Do not sell children short. Encouragement is an important tool to use to help them understand the value of trying, as, along with support, it assists in developing trust that is the cornerstone of a positive child/parent relationship.

Parenting *does* matter. Good parenting can have a serious impact on a child's goals, strategies, and personal philosophies. It is important to do the following:

Believe in the extraordinary potential of the child. Without faith, it is highly unlikely that any significant achievement will occur. With some children, success may require practice, memorization, and lots of patience, but the goal will be attained in all academic areas as well as in the arts, music, and science.

Developing Independence in Children

We all want happy children. There are times, though, when they cannot always feel happy. Teaching them how to tolerate and work through disappointment is an important job of parenting. With guidance, these are times that can help children grow in their emotional development.

It is through independence that children learn to feel good. Parents feel successful when they raise children who feel good and happy. However, problems may arise when independence is confused with happiness and feeling good. Some parents are too concerned with the child's feeling good, regardless of their child's behavior, which in many cases can result in narcissism. Narcissism is defined as excessive admiration of oneself and becoming overly preoccupied with what will make one feel good (i.e. having needs constantly met instead of trying to achieve needs independently). Parents create narcissism when they praise everything, even when the work or behavior is mediocre, and telling their child how wonderful they are without having truly earned the praise. Praise should be the result of a child's putting effort into doing something. Praise the effort as much as the result. Working hard to achieve a goal is worthy of praise.

Children who tend to develop narcissistic behaviors are:

- Demanding
- Feel they are special—more so than everyone else
- Cannot take responsibility for their own behaviors
- Have a grandiose sense of self-importance
- Expect to be recognized by everyone—parents, teachers, etc.
- Can't accept criticism by teachers or when graded down—this hurts their self-esteem
- Have fantasy of power, success, and ideal love
- Have less frustration tolerance that is given into by parents

Parents may become upset that the child is not made to feel good by other adults, teachers, etc. To overcome narcissistic behaviors, parents need to teach character and what types of behaviors and feelings are important in people. It is not only sports heroes, rock stars, etc. who have great character and are to be admired; it is people in everyday life who perform acts of kindness and friendship, and display care for others. These are the models we want to emulate.

Ways you can help your children develop independence:

- Allow your children to have their own thoughts. Explain why you think and feel the way you do, and encourage them to do the same. Let them stand up for themselves and let their voices be heard both in and out of school.
- Let them share their feelings when they are emotionally hurt so that they are in touch with their feelings, but not to the exclusion of others' feelings.

- Help them to be open to learning and new experiences and encourage them to work toward future goals that are not only focused on themselves.
- Support community giving and allow your child to experience the joy of making other people happy.
- Be sure your child has responsibilities that he/she must do regularly. Do not allow your child to conveniently get out of doing his/her responsibilities. The purpose of having responsibilities is to learn to be responsible when one is busy as well as free, hungry or full, tired or rested, motivated or lazy.
- Help your child to perceive reality without distortions.
- Help your child with problem-solving skills, but don't always "save" your child; it is the lesson learned from a struggle that children remember as they grow.
- Help them to stay with a task even though it may create frustration. Allow your child to struggle and cope with frustration.
- Value, praise, reward, and emphasize kindness, caring for others, and cooperation.
- Give your child opportunities to express increased self-control and to practice independent daily life skills. (What shall I wear today? What shall I have for dessert? Who shall I call for a play date? How can I amuse myself when I am alone?, etc.)
- Expect your child to be independent. Give him/her the tools needed (decision-making, communication, etc.) and then provide strong emotional support. Rejoice when things progress well. Be supportive when everything seems to fall apart.

- Give your child space and time to think, play with ideas, try new ways of accomplishing tasks and sharing his/her conclusions.
- Model the above behaviors to show your child that a happy life does include disappointments, limitations, mistakes, and obstacles, etc. as well as the "good stuff" that he/she has an abundance of.

It is important for parents to teach their children to identify with problems and solve them because life does have problems. Healthy children all have problems but know how to react to them. Children must learn to delay gratification and accept responsibility for chores and homework. They must be dedicated to truth by learning self-discipline and self-control. Parents should not dwell on accomplishments, but also emphasize human feelings and behaviors that they value:

- Self-Discipline
- Perseverance
- Responsibility
- Loyalty
- Work
- Courage
- Compassion
- Honesty
- Friendship
- Faith

Adults need to teach children that hard work and commitment to completing a task and trying to do one's very best is the way to feel good and proud. Sometimes it may take foregoing parties, play dates, etc. An important lesson to learn is that at times you cannot have everything you want and you can still feel good and happy. The goal is to have the good feelings come from within. For children, this is an ongoing process of development.

Developmental Approach to Parenting

Children love to learn. From infancy on, through the use of their senses, they are learning. Learning through all their senses—sight, sound, touch, smell, taste—precedes academic development. Naturally curious, little ones want to absorb new information. They want to learn, as it meets their needs and satisfies their curiosity and wondrous sense of discovery.

A developmental approach to learning takes into account all of a child's five senses and also their motor-systems and emotions. Emotions, which start off as a physiological system receiving input from the senses, affect what the child sees, hears, smells, touches, and feels, as well as where they move. They also help him/her to learn, mobilizing interest and motivation in the process. Then, from personal experience, emotions drive a child's interests in the world and create an internal life.

Understanding how emotions shape a child's mind into an integrated whole is the key to the developmental approach. Emotions affect the other parts of a child's life as well. Emotions not only mobilize interest and motivation, but also directly affect and orchestrate learning and achievement.

It is most important to recognize the role of emotions when children learn to use the natural gifts they are endowed with. Understanding how emotions shape your child's mind into an integrated whole is key when mastering this developmental parenting approach.

Children use their senses and motor-skills at each level of thinking. They learn to apply reason and thought to all of life's situations. These early years are when the building blocks are formed and critical abilities and skills develop.

Developmentally, knowing how a child, kindergarten-aged and up, learns to think can be evidenced by observing his/her play and everyday interactions with others. The kindergarteners' thinking skills need to be introduced into the curriculum.

Good, meaningful education should meet children where they are, providing experiences that will enable them to scale the educational ladder and be prepared for life. This will help them to become reflective thinkers, clear communicators, and organized problem-solvers in their families and at school.

It is important to help children master enough basic skills so that their motivation will take over. This enables them to enjoy and embrace the rich, complex world of ideas around them.

All children need time for reflection, play, and a flourishing parent-teacher partnership. When this partnership is characterized by steady, positive, productive, and trusting communication, everyone benefits.

Maxim: Educating a child needs to be viewed as a journey—not a race.

Developmental Stages, Tasks & Learning of Children's Psycho-Social Development

(reference Erik Erikson, Psychologist)

Birth to 1 year	Trust vs. Mistrust
2-3 years	Autonomy vs. Shame & Doubt
4-5 years	Initiative vs. Guilt
6-12 years	Industry vs. Inferiority
Adolescence	Identity vs. Role Confusion

Discipline

Discipline means to teach and have the child learn. The relationship that takes a lifelong approach will help children learn skills from impulses, managing angry feelings and considering the impact of their behavior on others. This practice comes from love, respect, and emotional connection. In this way, it can be an opportunity to connect with children in a positive way without being punitive.

Have you ever wondered if there is a time or an age when children will just do as they are told? Or have you ever wondered if there is a time or an age when children will just do what they know they are supposed to do? If so, you are not alone. Doesn't it make sense to expect that at some time children will just say, "Sure, Mom and Dad, I'll be happy to do what you ask right now. And I can't tell you how much I appreciate all you do for me."

Unfortunately, children seldom do what they are told to do by parents or do something just because they know they are supposed to. I don't even know of many adults who do this. Many of us eat things we know we aren't supposed to eat, are judgmental of others, even when we know we aren't supposed to be, may be late, tell little white lies, or procrastinate, even when we know we aren't supposed to. And we often resist requests from spouses—just because!

Just because what? Understanding why adults often resist a simple request might give us some clues as to why children resist. There are other factors for children, which will be addressed later, but first let's see what we have in common:

When a spouse asks you to do something, do you think or feel any of the following?

1. If I do what is requested, I'm letting my spouse control me.
2. Why should I do what my spouse requests when it is important to him/her, but doesn't matter to me? Why doesn't he/she lighten up and get a life?
3. Can't he/she see I have other things to do? Doesn't he/she think what I'm doing is important—and yes, that even means when I'm resting?
4. Why would I want to do anything when I'm asked in that tone of voice?
5. Who does he/she think I am—a slave?

Most of these issues have to do with <u>respect</u>. Spouses and children often feel a lack of respect when asked to do something. Later we will discuss how to increase our chances for cooperation by making requests respectfully. First we need to discuss the other reasons why children may not cooperate and do what they know they are supposed to do, even if the request is <u>respectful</u>.

1. Things they are supposed to do aren't high on *their* priority list—if they're on the list at all. Those things are on the adult's priority list. Children don't really care if the house is clean, if the lawn is mowed, if they are dressed on time, if they come to dinner on time,

etc. Does this mean they shouldn't do these things? No. For now, we are just discussing why they don't.

2. Children are individuating. This means they are in a continual process of finding out who they are—separate from their parents. How can they individuate without a little test of wills and boundaries, without trying the opposite of what their parents ask? The most profound spurt of individuation takes place when children reach adolescence, but smaller spurts occur throughout their growing years. Obedient robots will never become healthy, individuated adults.
3. And, of course, there is mistaken goal behavior when children don't believe they belong. Some children don't do what they are supposed to do as a way of getting undue attention, of showing misguided power, to get revenge for a real or perceived injustice, or because of assumed inadequacy. Parents are usually part of the problem when mistaken goal behavior is taking place, but it is usually children who get the blame.

Whatever the reasons, this is why a parent's job is never done. It is also why we need to keep using Positive Discipline methods over and over—because they are the most effective way to keep encouraging cooperation, even though it doesn't last forever. Dishes don't stay clean, beds don't stay made, and children don't always do what they know they are supposed to do. We can rage about this, or we can accept and find joyful ways to parent.

When children are sure of their parents' love, they can tolerate being disciplined. Accepting limits makes a child feel valued. Children will do better in school when parents are nurturing, high on structure, and show acceptance and firmness. The goal is to encourage a child's autonomy. Parents want their child to be happy—but also considerate, hardworking, and self-governing.

Positive Discipline Methods:

1. *Set expectations.* Hold children accountable to those expectations and respond to their mistakes (forgetting). This motivates and teaches your child to do what is right. This needs to be done with clear, firm expectations, not with anger.
2. *Set consequences.* Show them the seriousness of what they have done. For minor infractions, consequences should be immediate and not long-lasting. For major ones, the child needs to feel the seriousness, i.e. being grounded, no TV or other technology for a week or less. Ask the child what he/she feels is an appropriate consequence for what he/she did. This gives the child the ability to think more deeply about why the consequence is important to help him/her grow when they have doing something wrong. In addition he/she should do something right to make up for it. He/she should come up with something to help right the wrong. Consequences should be set during a time when there is not a present problem. This enables the child to know and understand the need for him/her to learn what is right and good and do what is right and good. Parental follow-through is essential to reinforcing your values and knowing what is appropriate for your child to incorporate into his/her own personality. A reminder about consequences is important to allow children to get

used to the idea of parents' consistent behavior when it comes to discipline—particularly when the child has gotten used to many chances and cajoling the parent to "give in."

3. *Set Limits.* One of the important aspects of setting limits is that we can see the value of the limits by observing what happens when they are not set. Many parents indulge their children in the name of love. In truth, indulging is one of the most unloving things we can do to our children. When things come too easily for children, they grow up thinking that the world owes them and they have no responsibility in giving back. When we give in to our children, we are teaching them to put all their intelligence and energy into learning how to manipulate others into taking care of them instead of learning to take care of themselves. Children need limits precisely in order to learn consequences. However, they need realistic limits. Setting limits can lead to emotional growth and independence. Children need limits at home, at school, and in public places. Limits provide security for a child. Knowing what one can do and cannot do gives children a better feeling of who they are and what the expectations are for their behavior. Most children respond well to a simple explanation of why parents say "no," particularly when it is for their own safety and the safety of others. When parents are clear as to dos and don'ts with a reasonable explanation, healthy children will accept the limit and understand that the love and acceptance of the parent is their security. The *need to please* is very important at all developmental stages for children before adolescence.

Children who test limits do so if the limit is not clear, the explanation is not clear, and/or the consistency in which the limits are given is not clear. *Consistency* and *clarity* is the mantra in dealing with children. Say what you mean and mean what you say.

There is a proven relationship between children's organized home life and school success. Observing scheduled homework time, bedtime, and regular meals at home prepares children to succeed in the structure of the school day. Some effective school strategies that parents can also use at home include:

- Don't confuse discipline with punishment. A child's home should not be like a boot camp. Convince children that limiting TV-watching and finishing homework assignments are in their best interests and are expected of all children.
- Explain your expectations. Make a list of rules and consequences that are clear, fair, and consistent.
- Encourage self-discipline. Regular schedules and routines help children remember what to do without being reminded or nagged, especially in getting ready for school, doing homework, and going to bed on time.
- Set a good example. When parents act responsibly at home and follow-up an established routine, their children are more likely to develop those same traits.

The kind of discipline a child receives should help the child regulate emotion in order to calm himself/herself down. Parents need to stay calm; the more emotionally aroused you are, the more aroused your child is likely to become. Hitting or screaming at a child results in anger and fear and interferes with the child's ability to care for others. In addition to avoiding physical punishment, children should never be threatened with a loss of love for misbehavior.

EMPATHY

Empathy is a key ingredient to a child's success in school and life. Manifestations of empathy often show up early in life, as when a toddler brings a favorite toy or blanket to another child who is injured or in distress. Some experts maintain that infants display empathy when they whimper or cry upon hearing another baby cry.

Children may enter the world with different capacities for empathy, a result of neural connections in the brain. The capacity for empathy may be partly or wholly lacking in disorders like autism and schizophrenia, in which the mind is focused inward.

But in otherwise normal children, the environment in which they are reared can make a big difference in whether empathy is fostered or suppressed. Healthy self-esteem is essential to empathy, so anything that helps children feel good about themselves will also help them recognize and respond effectively to the feelings of others.

If children are to relate positively to others, they must feel secure themselves and have a secure attachment to another person. Infants and young children whose own distress is ignored, scorned, or, worse yet, punished can quickly become distrustful of their environment and feel unsafe.

Children need a positive, caring relationship with their parents or caretakers if they are to be able to go beyond themselves to care about others. Empathy comes from being empathized with.

Children should also be helped to recognize their own feelings and express them. By learning to identify and label their feelings, children are better able to recognize the feelings of others. For example, when a child becomes frustrated with a toy car and throws it across the room, his caretaker could say something like: "You're feeling upset because the car isn't working the way it should. You don't like it when toys don't work."

Caretakers can help young children understand how other people feel by pointing out another child who is crying because their toy broke or was snatched by another child. When a child acts kindly toward someone, saying something like, "You're very kind for doing this" or "You're the kind of person who does nice things like that" can help make empathy a part of a young child's identity.

Even very young children need to know how their behavior affects others, experts say. They need to have it explained why certain behaviors are hurtful or helpful, and how to make up for bad behavior. You need to be really explicit, because children can't draw conclusions as easily as an older person.

Reading books and talking about how people (or animals) in a story feel and why they feel that way is helpful. One such book, *P.J. the Spoiled Bunny* by Marilyn Sadler, can help children appreciate the effects of being selfish and stubborn and always demanding one's way. The story helps children see how someone's actions affect the attitudes and responses of others. P.J. learns in the story that by behaving differently he could have more fun with his friends.

For older children, books like *To Kill a Mockingbird* and *The Diary of Anne Frank*—even televised events of natural disasters—can help by encouraging a child to imagine what it must be like for people whose lives are devastated by an earthquake or tsunami.

Although an early start is ideal, experts say it is possible to instill empathy later—even, for example, in children whose emotional security was neglected in an orphanage. Undoing the damage may require extra effort on the part of adoptive parents, as well as unconditional love.

Another way your child can learn to understand how others might feel is to role play. Help your child to see the perspective of the other person by helping him/her understand how he/she might feel in the same situation. To determine an emotional state of another person, for instance to recognize sadness in another, you need to identify the physical and verbal cues of sadness. Relate it to a similar experience they might have had or identify with a character in a story. "How would you feel if this happened to you?" Help them to imagine the stress that the other person might be feeling.

Parents can set a good example of empathetic behavior with how they behave themselves. The old saying "Do as I do" has particular relevance for fostering empathy in children. Parents should be models of altruism, compassion, and caring. It's not enough to talk the talk. You need to be seen showing caring behavior towards others and also to your child. By showing authentic and expressive concern for children as well as joy in their success, parents demonstrate how to be empathetic and create a caring environment in which children feel safe to show care and concern for others.

Family Life as it Affects Learning

Research supports that patterns of family life have a direct relation to success in academic learning.

The three significant practices that prevail in families are:

The Parent/Child Relationship

- Daily supervision of outside events
- Expression of affection
- Family discussion of books, newspapers, magazines, and television programs
- Family visits to museums, zoos, historical sites, and cultural activities
- Encouragement to try new words, expand vocabulary

Routine of Family Life

- Study time at home
- Daily routine that includes time to eat, sleep, play, work, study, and read
- A quiet place to study and read
- Family interest in hobbies, games, and activities of educational value

Family Expectations and Supervision

- Priority given to schoolwork and reading over television and recreation
- Expectation of appropriate manners, eye contact, etc.
- Parental expectation that children do their very best in learning—emphasis on "trying" rather than finished product for primary age. Upper-school-age need higher expectation for neatness, more in-depth research, organization, etc. Compliments for "trying" go a long way.
- Concern for correct and appropriate use of language
- Parental monitoring of children's peer group
- Monitoring and joint analysis of television viewing and internet usage
- Parental knowledge of child's progress in school and personal growth

Parenting *does* matter. Good parenting can have a serious impact on a child's goals, strategies, and personal philosophies. It is important to do the following: Believe in the extraordinary potential of your child. Without faith, it is highly unlikely that any significant achievement will occur. With some children, success may require practice, memorization, and lots of patience, but the goal will be attained in all academic areas as well as in the arts, music, and science.

Ways to Model Good Learning Habits:

Show your children that learning is a "Lifelong Process." Your children need the best start they can get. Parents need to make learning a family commitment. Show your children that you value education. Provide them with the resources they need. Make reading a priority. And never stop learning yourself. Show your children that learning never ends. Read. Write. Take a class. Try something new. Don't hesitate to say, "I don't know"—and then look up the answer together.

Put schoolwork to work. Let your children know you appreciate what they're learning and help them see its value. Point out how you use math when you do the family's finances, science when you cook, and reading for almost any task in your everyday life.

Open their eyes. Have a variety of reading material around the house, including books, magazines, reference materials, and newspapers. Show your children that you read for information as well as for enjoyment.

Read to them—big kids too. Don't stop reading to your children once they can read themselves. Read books to them that they're not quite ready to read on their own. It's a great way to spend time together, and they'll benefit from listening to higher-level and more involved stories with richer vocabulary.

Set up a zone. Make sure your children have a quiet, well-lit place to study at home, with reference materials and other school essentials close by. It's one of the most important ways you can help.

Encourage writing. Make up stories together. Have them keep a diary or journal or write to a faraway friend, relatives, or a pen pal.

Be descriptive. Broaden your child's vocabulary by using new and different words to describe the things around them. The air is frosty, icy, or frigid—not just cold. Be colorful in your descriptions. You'll be amazed at the difference it will make in their reading and writing.

Follow through. Children need to learn to be responsible. Teach them that when a job is assigned—whether it's homework or a household job—it's up to them to complete it. Make sure they understand the consequences if they don't get it done.

Don't accept second best. Don't let your children do anything less than their best work—no half-hearted efforts at homework or studying. Support and praise them when you see them hard at work.

Set and keep rules. Establish rules for behavior, at home, and at school. Let them know what will happen if they break those rules—they might be grounded, lose TV time, or have to do extra chores. Once you've set the rules, follow through every time. Consistency is key.

Aim high. Set high—but realistic—standards for your children, recognizing their unique strengths and weaknesses. Expect them to perform to the best of their ability—and they will.

Shoot for goals. Help your children set their own goals, whether it's improving their free throws or writing a creative story. It's essential for parents to set goals and expectations for their children. Teach them to aim as high as their abilities show.

Set priorities. Make schoolwork a priority. Expect them to get all of their homework, studying, and projects done before the TV, videogame, or computer ever gets turned on. Set and follow a schedule for schoolwork, reading, playing, meals, and bedtime.

Expect success. Let children know you're sure that they will be a success in school and in life. "I believe in you."

When a child comes to school prepared by attitude, habit, and skill to take the fullest advantage of the teacher's instruction, the teacher's own effectiveness is enhanced. We know that children learn best when their home environment includes the above patterns of family life. The partnership between home and school is necessary for the benefit of every child's success.

Family Life Can Affect a Child's Ability to Learn at School

Many young people complete their education with strong abilities to read, write, calculate, and apply disciplined thought for a solution to problems.

However, due to competition for children to learn more and excel in school, there is pressure to achieve in areas that individual students are not always available or ready to be challenged at in his/her stage of development.

There is much research dealing with a family's functioning, and influences on a child's adaptability to school and special ability to learning. Families that provide a stimulating, language rich, supportive environment and a family's relationships, practices, and patterns of life are more of a predictor of academic successful learning than a family's status.

Recommendations for a Parent–Child Relationship

- Daily conversations about everyday events both personal and global
- Expressions of affection
- Discussion of books, magazines, TV programs etc.

- Family visits to museums, zoos, historical sights, cultural activities, community volunteering that helps others to lead a good life
- Encouragement to continually try to use new words to expand vocabulary that can be used at home and at school as well as age-appropriate discussions about current events and other meaningful subjects

FAMILY EXPECTATIONS AND SUPERVISION

- Priority given to schoolwork during times when school is in session
- Parental expectations that encourage a child to try to do his/her best
- Parents monitoring of child's peer group
- Parents knowledge of child's progress in school and personal growth

In the twenty-first century, many research studies indicate that "emotional health in childhood is the key to happiness" vs. "academic achievement matters more than anything else for adult happiness."

"Money can't buy happiness" is a unanimous feeling by researchers. The question to ponder is "what is true happiness?" It is certainly not the same for every child. The old adage "know your child" applies since every child, even with the same parents, same siblings, and same environment each has his/her own personality and strengths.

Family Meetings

Good communication between parents and children is important for all families regardless of age, sex, or intelligence of its members. Family meetings create a climate of support where young people can develop the perceptions and skills necessary for successful living.

One of the main gripes that children have is that nobody listens to them—Mother and Dad don't listen, the nanny doesn't listen, teachers don't listen, and, in general, no one listens. These complaints have become so widespread that the feelings that youngsters have about people and authorities are immediately tainted and interfere with communication.

Educators and psychologists, as well as parents, are in a dilemma as to why children continually feel picked on, bitter, rejected, and unloved.

If we are to conscientiously explore the field of communication between parents and children and families, we need to examine our approach and method that we ourselves use in establishing communication within the family setting.

If we examine what this is all about, we find that we are, as a whole, a very vocal group of people. Whether we be American or European, Asian, Hispanic, or whatever our origin, we have learned how to talk *at* children rather than talk *with* them.

As parents and teachers, we face the problem of really knowing how to talk with and listen to young people.

Talking is a part of communication, listening is the very important other part—listening to what they have to say, not listening in terms of how many words they use, but really trying to hear what they are struggling to tell us.

Through the medium of a family meeting, we can begin to effectively listen to children and explore what they are trying to communicate to us. Meetings satisfy the need to feel important within the family by:

- Being listened to, not just heard, but understood
- Being taken seriously
- Feeling genuinely needed for one's personal worth, contributions, and significance

Structure is Security

In order for a child to gain from a family meeting, it is important that we legitimately allow expression of feelings from both parents and children.

However, in order to assure maximum success, it is important that we establish a structure within which children may comfortably express their feelings. Expressing feelings of anger such as "I hate you," "You're miserable," or "You're mean to me" really doesn't help the child grow in maturity and responsibility. Studies have proven that children verbalizing angry feelings truly doesn't add much to their ability to communicate. After a while, it seems to stir up anger in the adult who is on the receiving end of these expressions of anger. Once in a while, it is important for a child to be able to say strong things to a parent. It is important for a child to feel the parent can accept his saying "I hate you," etc. But when it becomes a pattern of relating, it doesn't allow the child to find better ways of coping with anger, and the freedom of expression becomes a vehicle for more anger and rejection for the youngster. Therefore, a structured, controlled, organized way of allowing children to communicate with their parents is the goal of the family meeting.

What happens when a family gets together?

Usually one or two members dominate the conversation. Under the plan of the family meeting, this can be controlled and adapted to the needs of the individual members of the family. In order for children to feel secure about such a meeting, there are rules that need to be established and followed.

Set a day and time for your family meeting. In order for it to be successful, it should be done weekly at the same time and same day. It should last between twenty and forty-five minutes depending on the age of the child. Usually the best time for meetings is on the weekends, Saturday or Sunday—the reason being, during weekdays, parents and children are tired and involved in many activities that are not family centered, and sitting down for conversation and trying to communicate might only add stress and strain to already tense moments. Try to allow no interference or distraction during the family meeting. Therefore, no other activity such as TV, computers, games, music, etc., should be going on. These distractions tend to make the meeting feel less important. Try to keep the day steady. Changing days cuts into the importance of continuity. Children are creatures of routine, and once routine is established they find strength and security in the consistency and dependability of the time, day, and activity.

Set an Agenda. Identify and pinpoint the topics or problems to discuss. Both parents should meet before the family meeting to discuss what should be emphasized. The discussions for each meeting should be chosen by consensus to help insure the success of the meetings.

Give children a chance to chair the meetings (after it has been successfully modeled by a parent). This is a good way to foster feelings of significance within the family.

Encourage everyone to participate with more than a one or two word answer. By participating in discussions, the children learn how to answer questions and give opinions more fully.

This is good vehicle for helping your children to learn how to reflect upon a situation. Don't rush the meetings. Give everyone a chance to think during a discussion. Ask questions such as "What do you think about what happened?" "What other things could you have done in that situation?" "Are you satisfied with the result? If not, Why?" "How can you do it differently if it comes up again?" And again, don't rush the answers. Give everyone plenty of time to think before they answer.

Sometimes issues may need to be tabled for next week if conflicts cannot be resolved—i.e. taking care of the dog and other issues involving responsibility, commitment, firmness, etc.

Returning to the same subjects is important—as with the issue of chores—some subjects need continual reminders and evaluation.

Provide special treats during meetings to provide a more relaxed and fun feeling. Creating good feelings about the family being together for meaningful discussions makes it easier for children to learn to communicate.

Family meetings in single parent families can be highly successful—the benefits are the same no matter how many are in the family.

Family meetings help children in a number of ways:

- They allow them to see a process being used to work through conflicts and to develop their higher-level coping skills.
- They help children learn how and why to make good choices.
- They help children develop tools to cope or deal with issues and to become more independent.
- They decrease immature behavior on the part of the child and help them develop a positive attitude about themselves as a family member and learner.

Gift of Reading

For your child's birthday, or over the holiday season, parents face many choices as to what gifts to give to their children. The dilemma is whether to give them what they want, to give them what they need, or to give them what you as a parent want them to want and appreciate.

A special gift you can consider is the gift of reading.

There have been studies showing a decline in the attention span of young children, as well as an adverse affect on a child's imagination, curiosity, prediction skills, and joy of discovery, all related to the rise of visual gaming over reading. Today's children have many diverting factors that provide other forms of instant gratification. However, it is important for children to sit with a book, smell the pages, have a tactile experience, and, of course, to sit back and dream as pictures appear in their minds.

Parents have the ability to model the enjoyment of reading. It is known that if parents are sitting and reading, then the children are reading too. If parents are staring at and absorbed in their phones and laptops, then the children will be staring at their devices as well.

Reading to children should start early and continue on as long as they are interested. Even as children get older, a parent reading to their older child about something that both find interesting plays an important part in developing listening skills, comprehension, and building vocabulary, and all of those play an important part in thinking and higher-level learning. The value of spending that time together can also not be overstated.

Some Tips for Parents:

- Experiment with audio books.
- Subscribe to children's magazines.
- Start a book club with other friends; meet weekly for sharing and discussion.
- Start a parent-child reading group. Read a chapter of a middle-grade book to younger children once a week. Read upper-grade books to older ones. Your children should discuss why it was funny or perhaps why it made us sad or wonder.
- Have family read time where all members of the family participate in reading and sharing a chosen part or a page to read and discuss. This leads to how, why, and what if questions to help develop comprehension and deep thinking.

As holiday seasons approach, help make them more meaningful by considering some of the above. You may find that sitting down and reading alongside your child turns out to be more enjoyable for you than you even imagined it could be. Being close together at holidays or other times provides many values to be grateful for—the values of caring love, warmth, and togetherness.

Reading is one of the most important skills that we can teach our children. In order to appreciate every other subject matter, they first must have the ability and confidence to read.

Goal Setting

Starting at age five or six, children need to learn to set goals. Under parental guidance all children can set appropriate goals for their age and development and put forth effort to attain them. It can be highly therapeutic, ego-building, and create important steps towards independence.

Explain that people choose goals dealing with things they want to change in order to make them and/or their families happier. Goal setting doesn't have to be a continual struggle for improvement. It's good for children to see their past accomplishments and feel good about those, and then maybe set a goal to try something new as they continue to grow on each new birthday. Offer a few suggestions as to what they might want to work towards or character traits that you see could use some improving.

Encourage them to talk about what they want to have, achieve, and earn. The decision-making process allows children to establish a sense of identity and form their own aspirations. Real motivation for self-improvement comes from within.

External rewards can be most legitimate for elementary-age children. Earning a specific reward for effort on one's part has a definite affect on self-esteem and independence. It could be a gratifying experience for both parents and child. It is a positive way of emphasizing "I can do" and therefore deserves praise, as well as a tangible reward—not always a new toy, but a privilege of staying up later, going out to a special dinner, a trip to a museum, or fun experiences like a special sleepover, etc. However it needs to be of high interest to motivate a child to want to put forth the effort to earn parental praise and celebration with a reward. Motivation for self-improvement will eventually move from external to internal as maturity continues to grow and develop.

Step by Step Goal Setting:

- At the beginning of the week, identify one challenging but attainable goal. Some ideas could be: getting ready for school and being there on time; getting ninety percent correct on the weekly spelling test; doing homework and reading nightly; preparing for a book report, etc.
- Write the goal down on a piece of paper. Post it on the refrigerator or bulletin board.
- Talk about how to accomplish the goal. Break it down into small steps—you could pack your lunch at night, set the alarm clock fifteen minutes earlier so you can get to school by 8:10 a.m. and not rush into class, or have a special place and time for homework each day, etc.
- As the week progresses, check to see how things are going. If problems arise, talk about possible solutions. If your child is falling behind in studying spelling words, you might set up a ten-minute nightly review. If reading a book for a report, talk about a particular chapter, etc.
- At the end of the week, help your child evaluate how well he/she did. Was the goal achieved? Why or why not?

Encourage your children to talk about the evidence of their success or failure on fulfilling their goals. Children can only benefit when they are helped to see that clear goals, motivation, and effort on their part is essential to help them attain them. Give them lots of opportunities to practice and to succeed. This skill, of setting and achieving goals, is crucial for future lifelong success.

Good Judgment/Good Decisions/Good Choices

Children develop strong character by learning to think about and make sound judgments about what is right or wrong, good or bad. These are not always easy distinctions for adults to make, much less children.

For example, it can be difficult for a child to recognize the difference between acting bravely and acting recklessly. As parents, we can help by showing, through what we do as well as what we say, that it is important in such situations to think carefully and honestly about what should be done, carefully weighing how others will be affected by what we do.

Sometimes we get into trouble because we "just didn't think." We let our emotions lead us to actions that we regret later. Making good judgments requires skills in monitoring impulses, using reasoning to sort through feelings and facts, and thinking about the consequences of our actions.

Your child's ability to think and make sound judgments will improve as he/she matures. With age, however, it also may become easier for him/her to try to justify and make excuses for selfish or reckless behavior. However, if you have helped him/her develop strong habits of honesty, courage, responsibility, and self-respect, your child will have the ability to see the flaws in his/her reasoning and be able to come to the right conclusion about what to do.

How to Help your Child with Good Judgment:

- Teach your child to stop and think before acting on impulse.
- Teach your child to tell fact from feeling. Let him/her know that just because he/she feels strongly about something—such as hitting someone who made him/her angry—doesn't mean it's the right thing to do.
- Encourage your child to think about the consequences of his/her decisions. Tell him/her little stories about situations he/she might face and talk about actions he/she might take, who might be affected by his/her actions, what might happen because of his/her actions, and what the best action might be.
- When your child has a problem with a rule, brainstorm together a list of possible reasons for the rule. This leads to greater understanding.
- Remind your child to pay attention to the rules or codes that apply in each situation. For example, the rules for behaving in church are different from those for a football game.

How to Help your Child Make Good Decisions:

All children need to learn how decisions they make can affect them as they learn and interact with others. Obviously, good decisions bring happiness and good feelings, and poor decisions bring unhappiness, anger, and frustration. As children learn that there are consequences for their decisions, they begin to see the importance of making good ones.

As early as kindergarten age, children learn to understand how their decisions can affect their feelings about themselves as well as others (i.e. saying 'please," "thank you," and listening to the teacher brings about a smile, a pat on the head, or a compliment from the adult.) In contrast, not listening or bothering a friend can result in a consequence of time out on the playground and not being able to join in the "fun of playing."

With older children, a poor decision may result in the consequence of loss of privileges at home (i.e. not having a sleepover, etc.).

In other words, *decision- making* and *consequences* are compatible values. Learning an affect of one's behaviors is an important developmental task throughout elementary grades. It is a readiness skill that will serve them well in adolescence.

How to Help your Child Make Good Choices:

All children need to know that they have choices as to how to respond when someone teases or excludes them, or excludes others when they are included. Starting as early as kindergarten, we teach children about dealing with conflicts through the use of *choice*,— "please stop," "ignore it," "talk it over," or "ask the teacher for help."

As children progress in the grades, teachers employ role-playing, group discussions, and class meetings to empower students to find ways of dealing with issues that create helplessness. We continually help children to see that they have power to deal constructively when their feelings are hurt. They are experiencing pain and need to find healthy expressions to replace it.

At home, parents can be proactive in helping children make appropriate choices. Family meetings in which issues are discussed that involve family members in helping with chores, getting along, sharing with one another, and experiencing feelings about family rules and decisions are important times for children to feel they have a choice in working out solutions, with the guidance of their parents, for whatever conflicts arise. This empowers children to move into more independence, while developing tools to cope or deal with issues and accept responsibility. Being part of the process to work through conflicts and arrive at solutions increases maturity and helps children move on to higher level coping skills. Solving problems for them without their input creates helplessness and fosters increased immature behavior.

Use the word "choice" regularly as you talk to your child:

- "Good choice to include Mary in your game!"
- "Let's think about what other choices you could have made before you used your hands on a friend."
- "Which choice did you make when you were frustrated and angry with John?"

Just as we are all concerned about developing academic and physical growth in school, of equal importance is creating opportunities for them to grow in their ability to adjust to, cope with, and solve problems.

GRATITUDE

The Thanksgiving holiday should not be the only day we focus on being grateful for all we have and the many blessings that pour into our lives day by day, moment by moment.

It is said that "Gratitude unlocks the fullness of life. It turns what we have into enough and more. It turns denial into acceptance, chaos into order, a house into a home, stranger into friend. Gratitude makes sense of our past, brings peace for today and creates a vision for tomorrow."

It is important to hug your family and friends and let them know you care and are grateful for their being part of your daily life.

Practicing gratitude at a young age promotes later development of self-control and self-regulation, which are resources for lifelong success.

Research further confirms that gratitude helps foster positive emotions, and those emotions help children with the learning process—by keeping the stress level down.

We need to help children realize that there are good things in the world—the many gifts and benefits that they receive. They need to recognize that these sources of goodness came from *others* to make *us* feel good.

When parents practice gratitude in their own lives so that it becomes a part of who they are, the easier it is to model it for their children.

Happiness

Happiness cannot be felt all the time by anyone. Life is full of ups and downs. But with children, we certainly hope that they feel happy more times than not. And we all want our families to be happy and to have good feelings shared by all members.

There are a couple of practices that can help children focus on being happy so that they become aware of what actually does make them happy. These tools can then also help after a child has worked through something that they struggled with, or after they worked through sensitive issues with friends or other family members and are in need of some cheering up.

The Happiness List

Ask your child to write down five things that happened yesterday that made him/her feel happy. They should be the first five things that come into his/her mind. Especially have them think of the small things that they usually don't notice that might have put a smile on their face. For example, you might prompt them with some of the following questions: Did the sun shine today? Did your teacher give you a complement? Did your friend say something nice to you? Did you get a new pet? Were your new shoes comfortable?

Try to do this every day. It will become a habit and will help your child look for and think about things that make him/her happy even though they may not have thought about it before. Have your child write or tell you their list at bedtime, and record it in a special notepad. It has to become easy to remember good things that happen to you.

Five reasons to keep the Happiness List everyday:

- It will give your child the power to think positively.
- It shows your child that they make their own happiness.
- It shows your child how they can choose to do things to fully experience life.
- It helps them to look deeply for things to make them feel happy.
- It teaches them how to collect and store good feelings.

The Happiness Book

To promote family happiness, create a special "Happiness Book" and have each member of the family create one page every weekend. Each member of the family should create a page that shows what his/her ideas are about what happiness is that day and then share it with the other members of the family. A little celebration with favorite snacks or food will add to it to make it a special occasion.

There are many variations to this idea with the goal of encouraging all members to think positively, act positively, and enjoy and share their good feelings with others.

Homework

Homework Affects Achievement in School

As a parent, it's important for you to know that homework really can make a difference in your children's performance at school. The time spent doing homework directly affects a child's achievement. This is important information. It tells us that by doing assigned homework, children will increase skills and do better in school. Some recent findings:

- Students who consistently do homework perform better academically than those who do not do homework.
- By doing homework, students can improve academic achievement in all subjects.
- Homework improves academic achievement at all grade levels, both elementary and secondary.
- Doing homework improves academic achievement of both high and low achievers.

When you help your children do their homework appropriately, you are helping them improve academically. Through homework, you have the daily opportunity to make your children more successful.

Homework teaches your children responsibility.

How to Appropriately Nurture your Children

Children face many challenges in their roles as students. Each day brings new encounters and risks. It is amazing to think of the influence parents and educators have on their lives. This places much responsibility on us to use our influence wisely.

In order for learning to become meaningful and successful, there needs to be appropriate nurturing. Nurturing is not only proactive and loving care, it is also showing a child you have confidence and trust in his/her ability to handle learning challenges and social situations. These are the most important elements in helping to develop and create an independent child.

Allowing children to confront challenges, interpret them, and decide on how to approach the resolution gives them feelings of confidence in themselves. Through independent experiences, children can construct how they will function in the world as confident and independent individuals.

Nurturing needs to take place in the emotional and intellectual realms. Knowing that we live in an information age, we need to help children discern what is important for them to learn and how to use technology wisely. High priority must be given to morals and values as well as knowledge about basic skills and the world around them. As children begin to think critically and on their own, they will eventually be able to screen out information that is not age appropriate or confusing. Before then, we owe it to them to help them learn how to make good decisions, how to use their acquired information wisely, and to guide them into becoming productive beings.

Importance of Kindness

In an increasingly complex world, simple kindness can have a long-lasting, positive effect, especially on children who experience its power early on in their lives. The trait of kindness must be nurtured and encouraged in all children by the adults who care for them each day so that this quality will remain with them as they enter adulthood. Teaching kindness to our children can connect them to parents, teachers, their communities, and the entire world!

We have all observed how easily and genuinely kindness flows from children—the sharing of favorite foods or flowers picked from the garden, the offering of toys, and the sincerely-felt concern over hurts suffered by others. Simple acts of kindness are natural to children.

When we make the extra effort of being kind when we aren't expected or required to and surprise someone, including ourselves, that is a "random act of kindness"—a good deed that is truly the embodiment of compassion and caring.

Simple Definitions that Kids Understand

- *Random:* A kind act is "random" when it is unexpected—done for no reason and without expecting anything in return.
- *Random Act of Kindness:* When we do a random act of kindness we give for the sake of giving; we act simply out of the goodness within us.

- *The Chain of Kindness*: When you do something kind for someone, that person feels so good about what you did, he or she does something kind for someone else and the kindness becomes a chain reaction, moving from one person to the next.

This can be as simple as finding something and returning it to its rightful owner; it might be an "act of kindness" for a needy neighbor. Maybe your child needs to make some extra effort to be kind to a less "popular" child. The task may be very small, but the ramifications are huge. These are the moments when a child learns kindness and compassion, when he/she develops a much stronger sense of self and comes to understand who he/she is in the world. These "Acts of Kindness" make a deep impression on a child's needs. It can have an everlasting effect on one's personality and memory of how one feels when doing something for another person.

You don't have to go searching for such moments in your own life. There is always a person in need, someone who needs a kind word, a helping hand. It doesn't have to be as big as cooking a homemade meal for a sick friend. In fact, small kindnesses that require little thanks or recognition are just as important as the larger good deeds. The important thing is that we capture those moments when we can show our children what kindness and compassion is, and help them add that to the skills and understanding that will guide them through adulthood.

I'm Sorry— Better Strategies for Apologizing

Apologies of "I'm sorry" are used too often as children learn how to terminate a conflict, get out of trouble, an excuse for not getting punished, or even not telling the truth. "I'm sorry" without the feeling of remorse can only perpetuate the apology and develop a pattern of behavior for people of all ages—not only children. It truly affects the character of a person and motivation to change the situation that was created.

In order for parents to respond to children's issues with others, they can consider this plan:

I'm sorry for hurting (another person's feelings).
This is wrong because (I really want to be friends, etc.).
In the future I will (use my words to communicate my genuine apology).
Will you forgive me? (What might I do to let you know I'm really your friend?)

You can even make a poster at home entitled "How to Say I'm Sorry."

The most important thing is that the apology must be sincere—really mean you're sorry and the other person will experience your caring about what happened to his/her feelings. The goal is to develop empathy, create a positive feeling, reduce angry feelings, and say proactive words that are positive: "I really want to be your friend." "I truly am sorry I hurt your feelings." "Please give me a chance to show you I really mean it."

It's difficult to break patterns of rote "I'm sorry." It takes patience and caring to help the child make a change and try a new approach that you will endorse as a better way to show care about family members and friends. Give it time and much reinforcement to really make it a part of your child's character.

Incentives and the Concept of "Earning"

Many child development authorities, as well as parents, agree that in general children tend to be overindulged in middle class urban society—overindulged in terms of being given "things" and experiences they may not be ready for at a particular age and/or stage of development; too much, too soon.

Because young children are highly responsive to concrete and material things, i.e. toys, games, etc., it can become too easy to lavish goodies on them, which in turn can evolve into demanding and unlovable behaviors.

Maturation of children can certainly be increased and accelerated when they feel that they have the power to earn things, which in turn provides a vehicle for increased self-concept and wanting to grow.

Rewards or incentives motivate children to work or try for something that can be earned through effort and energy on their part. In contrast to "bribery," where something is given for effort not expended or earned, rewards or incentives can become strong and important motivational forces to encourage effort in areas where there may be conflict.

Every child has something important and meaningful that he/she could earn, e.g. extra TV time, a special bedtime, a special trip, time alone with mom or dad, as well as games, toys, etc. Parents can use these things to set goals, daily, weekly, or monthly, by which children can "earn."

This can prove gratifying enough to the child so that it will eventually create independence, more self-control, and intrinsic motivation, all leading to good feelings about himself/herself. Children need to feel that growing up is important, exciting, and advantageous. All children want "things." What better way of giving to them than through "earning." Let's put "earning" into every child's vocabulary.

Keeping Children Healthy— Colorful Plant Foods

The research on nutrition and good health shows that colorful plant foods can have a powerful effect in our diets. Colorful plant foods provide nutrients and antioxidants that go into the cells of our brain, heart, and other organs and protect them from wear and tear. This can help in the prevention of many diseases.

Children will tend to try new foods when they come in bright reds, greens, blues, purple, orange and yellow. Make a plan to eat some brightly colored plant food every day. By eating different colors throughout the week, a variety of nutrients will enter your body.

<u>A Fun Idea:</u>

Since most children are responsive to games, here are some variations on a theme that can help to promote healthy eating of colorful plant foods.

- Set up a weekly chart that lists the different colorful plant foods that your family could eat for that week.
- Every day, place a check or star next to the plant food that was eaten that day.

- An extra star can be given to a plant food that is not listed.
- Predict the amount of different plant foods that can be eaten for the week.
- The person who comes the closet to the number predicted for the week has the privilege of selecting a treat, food, or fun activity for the entire family to experience.
- The goal is to make it a habit to eat plant foods daily and weekly to promote healthy eating habits.

Keys to Success—Trying and Hard Work

Self-esteem is enhanced as children learn to master academic skills in the core curriculum (reading, language skills, math, etc.). In addition, social and emotional successes play a significant role in their overall development. It's important that we move beyond the concern with self-esteem, especially when its quest undervalues hard work and discipline. For some children, learning is not always a happy process, but learning does bring satisfaction, especially when the end result is tangible. Parents as well as children need to discover and build on their "strength"—an academic area, social skill, music, art, drama, or sports, etc. This "strength" needs to be continuously bolstered while the weaker areas can be addressed. The success of enhancing ones strength can lead to positive self-esteem and motivation to improve in other areas. This is a process that takes time, effort, and energy but is an achievable goal.

When we ask children to clean their rooms, complete a reading assignment, memorize multiplication tables, be kind to someone, practice an instrument, or try a little harder to do their best, we do so because we want them to create certain habits of their hearts and minds. The memory of a job well done or of getting it right will create its own enticement and expectation and ultimately an internalized sense of quality.

Parents need to continue to encourage children to "try" to do their very best. Children need to learn what is their "very best" in a variety of activities in addition to reading, writing, and math. It needs to permeate all that they do—sports, music, art, homework, etc. Parental encouragement is most beneficial when it focuses on the *effort*—not the *result*.

TRYING and *HARD WORK* are the keys to success as children move on to lifelong learning and living.

Listen to Your Children

Forget the old-fashioned notion that children should be seen and not heard. Today, we know that "actively" listening to children is an important parenting skill. But there is more to the art of effective listening that meets the ear. Many parents are often too busy lecturing their children to truly listen...or they only pretend to listen.

Parents who listen well to their children may reap many rewards. Perhaps the most important of these is that listening enables parents to really know and enjoy their children. Improved behavior is another reward because children who are heard don't have to use inappropriate means to capture parental attention. Listening is also one of the best ways to show your child love, respect, and attention.

It does take time and effort to "actively" listen with undivided attention and to give encouraging responses. But with a few practical guidelines, even the busiest parents can find time to listen to a child who feels he/she has something important to say. Here are some tips.

Be Considerate

If it's the "wrong" time or you're busy, say so—but set a time when you can listen. Bedtime is a favorite time for youngsters to bring up serious topics, and if your child is not overly tired, it can also be a good time for a heart-to-heart talk.

Honesty Pays Off

If you are uneasy talking about a topic or don't know the answer, admit it. It may be more appropriate to refer your child to a teacher, another family member, or the internet. If your mind wanders for a moment, ask the child to repeat what he/she said. If you become distressed, call a timeout and resume the conversation after you calm down.

Don't Interrupt

Let your child speak without breaking in, especially if the conversation is heated. Do not finish sentences or provide words for them.

Pay Attention

Be calm and maintain eye contact. Don't show your impatience by drumming your fingers on the table, repeatedly looking at your watch, shaking your foot, or watching TV.

Really Listen

Concentrate on hearing and understanding what your child is saying instead of planning what you are going to say when it's your turn to talk.

Give Feedback

Encourage your child to keep talking with comments like: "How nice!" "Oh no!" or "Then what happened?" Smile and use appropriate gestures, such as a sympathetic shrug or nod.

Make Eye Contact

Watching your child's body language and facial expressions will increase your understanding of the message. This is especially important with younger children since some have limited vocabularies in kindergarten and lower grades.

Be Courteous

Avoid raising your voice, expressing anger, or humiliating your child. Save grammar or punctuation corrections for another time. Stick to the subject your child has asked to discuss. Provide answers or give advice only as needed.

Acknowledge the Message

Even if you disagree, make it clear that you have heard and understood the message. If you did not understand, ask questions. Paraphrase or summarize the message to show that you "got it."

LISTENING is part of PAYING ATTENTION—a skill every student must develop to the fullest in order to learn and achieve success.

Partnership Between Home and School

A true partnership between the parent, teachers, and administrators benefits the growth and development of each student. A child's needs are best met through a successful partnership. It is a relationship that is built upon trust, on steady, positive, and productive communication, and on supporting the importance of your child and their education. There are numerous, concrete, and not-too-time-consuming ways that parents can help their child succeed in school. I offer several possibilities in the following. Find the ones that work best for you, your family, and your child so that together we can show your child how important their education is to you.

How Can You Help Your Child Become More Successful in School?

Take time to make time

One key to success is to follow a schedule. Children need a schedule they can depend on—one that includes definite times for homework, meals and sleep. They then can work around those times to include the extras.

Limit TV and video games
Decide how much of this kind of free time to allow—and stick to it. Otherwise, these activities can consume too much of children's time.

Read, read, read
Continue to share reading with children, even after they can read by themselves. This allows them to enjoy stories that may be too difficult for them to read alone. Discussion of stories and characters is important.

Show interest
Take time to look at work your child brings home from school. You will see work that teachers feel is important enough to send home. Talk about the schoolwork together. If it's a test, talk about how to improve the grade, etc. This shows that you care about the things your child spends most of the day doing.

Go for the goals
If you want to help your child form a habit that brings lifelong success, you can—by teaching the importance of setting and reaching goals. These tips can help you get started: Ask your child to think of a school subject she/he wants to improve in (perhaps a math skill, such as multiplication). If it's important to her/him, she's more likely to try. Talk about ways your child can reach her/his goal—one step at a time. Then, help her/him set up a schedule. Can she/he learn three multiplication facts daily, practice with speed drills, or create a times table to study?

Point out your child's efforts along the way
Example: "You spend a lot of time working out the examples. That's what it takes to improve."

Help your child imagine what it will feel like to reach her goal
Example: Picture yourself breezing through these multiplication problems once you know all the facts.

Problem? Try the team approach
What can you do if you don't agree with how a teacher is handling a problem? First, try talking with the teacher. There may be another side of the story you haven't heard. It's best to avoid giving your child a feeling of a separation between school and home in front of the child so that they don't develop a negative attitude toward school. Instead, you can teach respect by working with the teacher—together you can come up with a great solution. It is a good model for children to see and be involved in working through a problem that they benefit from. Good communication between teachers and parents benefits the child.

Ways That You Can Make a Difference in Your Child's Education:

Be a Positive Influence.
Your attitudes and actions influence your child at home and at school.

Encourage, don't discourage.
Praise your child's efforts, and boost his or her self-esteem. Avoid making negative statements, such as, "You're not very good at math." Emphasize the strengths he/she exhibits in

other areas to help develop an acceptable performance in spite of a weakness.

Help your child be independent.
Teach him/her to budget time and make decisions. Encourage your child's interest in hobbies and activities.

Set goals together.
Format, plan how to reach goals. Be realistic—don't expect more (or less) than your child can do. Chores need to be part of family living.

Talk positively about school.
Talk about teachers and classes/subjects you liked. Talk positively about friendships and how to maintain friends. And, make sure your child goes to school every day.

Be a positive role model.
Teach by example. Develop healthy habits that can be shared, such as cooking healthy meals and exercising together, from walking to higher-level equipment, etc.

Show your love.
Let your child know that you love him/her. Avoid comparing your child to others, especially brothers and sisters or friends who have higher levels of ability.

Spend time with your child.
Go on walks or picnics, visit museums, etc. Spend time with your child and his/her friends, too. Know how to respect his/her privacy.

Talk with your child.
But don't talk "at" him/her. Ask questions, and listen carefully.

Make your home a good place to learn.

Build good relationships with your child's teacher, administrators, and other staff members.

Get involved in your child's school life.

Encourage your child with praise, guidance, and love.

How Parent Involvement in School Helps:

We have learned from substantial research that students' accomplishments are highly linked to parents' involvement in school events, especially when they involve themselves in the life and learning of their children.

Most importantly, it is crucial for parents to understand and respect the school's values and support them in the home. A school's core values and expectations need parent support and cooperation to be effective in the growth and development of children.

When parents attend assemblies, performances, back to school night, sporting events, and the like, they are giving their children a message: "We are interested, we care about you and your school, we follow what is happening, we know that teachers and administrators are pleased to know you, understand and recognize your abilities and uniqueness as well as other special things about you."

Ways Parents Can Foster a Positive Work Ethic in Their Children:

- Remind children that much of what they accomplish results from their *effort* and dedication, not their innate ability.
- Teach them that their *ability is not finite and limited,* but is instead a resource to be expanded through practice.
- *Praise your child* with such phrases as "Look how much you can learn when you try hard" or "Your effort really paid off."
- Model and share your work ethic. *"Shoot for the moon. Even if you miss it, you will land among the stars!"*

How Busy Parents Can Help Children Succeed in School:

Recently, researchers were surprised to learn that when asked if they wanted more time or money most people answered, "More time." But sometimes it can be a matter of using time more efficiently. Here are a few suggestions to hopefully help you see how you can begin to use some of your time more effectively:

Use time in the car

with children of any age, or even bath time with young children, to squeeze in a little more learning and to talk about specifics about school. Of course, your child can't read library books in the tub—but he can repeat the addition facts. He can't write an essay in the car—but he can talk about what he's going to write or perhaps review spelling words.

Set priorities.
Decide what's really important to you. (Odds are, it's your kids.) Then, consciously decide how to spend your time. Make sure your decisions reflect what matters. Have a choice between cooking a fancy dinner or reading with your child? Order a pizza and read the book.

Spend one-on-one time.
Children need both 'quality' and 'quantity' time. But, there's nothing like spending time alone with a parent to make a child feel special. Every week, make an appointment to spend some time alone with each child. Get out your calendar and enter it. Then treat that appointment as seriously as you would an important business meeting.

Remember the 80/20 rule.
Businesses often use something they call the "80/20 rule." Simply stated, it means that eighty percent of the results of any job come from just twenty percent of the effort. Use this rule as you decide how to spend your time. Instead of just "doing things right," you'll start "doing the right things."

Volunteer after hours.
You don't always have to come to school during the day to help your child's school. Here are some things you can do at home or after school:

- Collect and send in materials the teacher needs for a class project.
- List community resources that support what the class is studying.

- Take care of the class guinea pig or other pets during a vacation.
- Type students' papers so they can be "published" as books.
- Prepare food from a country or culture the class is studying.
- Recruit other parents to volunteer.
- Enlist businesses to donate to a school fundraiser and/or give matching funds for a donation.

How Parents Can Help Boost a Child's Attention Span:

Children who can pay attention have the most success in kindergarten. They will know how to listen when someone is speaking or reading a story.

Here's how to help if you think your child has difficulty paying attention:

- *Give your child short tasks*, such as putting together a puzzle of four pieces, or coloring part of a picture. When done, say, "You did it!" The more success he/she has, the more he/she will learn to pay attention. Make tasks longer as his/her attention span increases.
- *Try using a kitchen timer*. Many children work better if they have a cue. "I'm going to set the timer for ten minutes. I want you to make shapes from this clay until you hear the timer go beep."
- *Keep work areas free of clutter*. Most children find it easier to concentrate without too many objects around them.
- *Tell your child what you expect*. "We are going to read a storybook now. I need you to sit next to me and look at the book while I read."

Parent Conferences:

Conferencing with parents is an important time to find out more specifically how your child is adjusting to his/her social, emotional, physical, and ever-important development. Some important questions and suggestions that will help you gain a satisfactory and insightful understanding of your child are as follows:

- Ask your child if there is anything that he/she would like you to discuss with the teacher.
- Jot down everything that you want to talk about at the conference.
- Begin with positive comments about your child's attitude toward school and his/her likes or dislikes.
- Avoid lengthy discussions of topics that are not related to the purpose of the conference.
- Be open to suggestions and recommendations from the teacher.
- Take notes about what has been discussed and share them with your child when it is time for him to participate.
- Be aware of the limitations of time and other parents' needs as well as your own.
- What skills and knowledge will my child be expected to master next?
- What will my child learn this year in math, science, history, and English that I can help by supplementing at home?
- Are there challenging academic standards in place?
- How do you balance basic skill development and enrichment?

- How is my child evaluated?
- What kind of information do you use to evaluate students?
- How do you know if a child is working up to his/her potential?
- How are grades determined in your classroom?
- What can I do to stay more involved in my child's academic progress?
- What can I do at home to complement what is happening in the classroom?
- How can I support teachers' efforts in implementing higher academic standards?
- How do you accommodate differences in learning?
- How is my child's learning style and ability being met?

Both parents and teachers should look forward to the conference time as a true learning experience for both.

Some Thoughts for Parents to Consider:

A parent's language is a powerful tool. Our language can build a child up or tear him/her down. It can model respectful and caring social interactions or do just the opposite. Effective language supports children in their learning rather than criticizing them for their mistakes. Every child needs encouragement just as a plant needs water to grow. It is the parent's persistent encouragement that helps a child reach the next highest level.

Educators are aware that children cannot learn well when they are fearful of making mistakes. Even in a non-threatening environment, some children are fearful about many things in or outside of school. Therefore, it is so very important for parents to constantly cushion their children against anxieties with reminders and support.

Parents need to be aware that realistic expectations for performances should not be confused with pressure. Parents and teachers need to be positive in creating a feeling of "you can do it when you try your best." Accomplishment and success have a direct effect on self-esteem. All human beings need good feelings and support from adults to grow and be successful in life. It all begins in childhood.

A reminder about homework: Before each assignment, reinforce learning truths about mistakes! Try to include some of these points as you "help" your child. It is important to help your child to not develop a perfectionist style.

- "As you do your homework, remember, you don't have to do everything perfectly. Just try your best."
- "Making mistakes is how we learn. Making mistakes shows you are trying and taking risks. Children learn more when they are willing to take risks."
- "As your mother (or father) I appreciate your trying even if it is hard. I understand how you feel when you think you can't do something and it needs to be done right."
- Long-range assignments for upper grades require help in time management—to guide your child in the importance of anticipating what needs to be done, how long it will take, and strategies needed to be successful through completion of the task. Teachers need to be available to help parents with specific approaches to use for each student's grade level.

Parents and Their Child's Learning:

As parents, you need to understand that your children cannot and will not always be successful in their learning, and that weaknesses can be opportunities and failures can open doors. Never sell your children short, and, instead, encourage them. Your support is an important tool. It is always a positive to make things easier for your child, and building trust with him/her is also critical, as it aids in your youngster's learning and development. Trust-building starts in the very early years and continues throughout the elementary ones. When you give your child your unconditional faith and support, you put him/her in a position to successfully cope with the issues of adolescence that lie ahead, and you strengthen your parent/child relationship.

It is equally important for you to believe in your child's extraordinary potential. Without your faith, it will be difficult for them to thrive, but with *your* encouragement, patience, and realistic goal-setting, and *their* practice, memorization, and perseverance, they will be much more likely to attain their goals in music, art, science, and more.

A Few Final Tips for a Successful Partnership:

Before talking to other parents about anything that has to do with the classroom, please talk to your child's teacher. It is a simple courtesy that should be afforded to the teachers.

If your child is having difficulty with another child in school, encourage your child to speak to the other child first. If there is no satisfactory resolution, they should then approach the teacher. Calling other parents tends to intensify the situation and may not be helpful. The principal or head of school should be advised when the conflict cannot be resolved. Remember that your child will tell you about conflicts at school from his/her point of view. All of us shade stories by telling the parts that are most sympathetic to our point of view. Do not assume that all of the problems are caused by another child. Keep talking and always ask, "What did you do that might have caused this conflict? What didn't you do that could have avoided this conflict?"

Be positive about your child's placement—children are savvy and can read their parents' emotions. (Have faith and trust in the teachers and administrators.)

Get your information from the right source, which will not be found in the carpool line. It's best to have your facts straight before you email a teacher.

Please do not gossip or talk negatively about other children.

When you child comes home excited by learning or about something that happened at school, don't hesitate to send your teachers a note or email—your feedback means so much.

Perfectionism—How Parents Can Help

Children who have perfectionist tendencies can have difficulty functioning in the classroom because their expectations for themselves are so high that completing or even attempting schoolwork is hindered. This can result in low self-esteem, chronic feelings of inadequacy, decreased performance, and increased tension and anxiety. Perfectionism has been linked to crippling performance anxiety (such as stage fright), psychosomatic disorders (such as headaches), depression, and suicidal behavior. It can emerge into an obsessive-compulsive personality disorder in adulthood.

This trait is common in gifted children and seems to result from a desire to be considered best in all situations. As a result, a gifted child may refuse to try activities rather than risk failing to achieve a superior level of performance, and consequently fall into a pattern of underachieving. Gifted children who attempt to be perfect in all aspects of their lives are also susceptible to burn-out. Perfectionism can also be seen in non-gifted children. It can be particularly problematic for a learning-disabled student.

Unfortunately perfectionism has the opposite of its intended effect. Rather than saving the child from criticism and gaining love and approval, perfectionism hinders both achievement and social relationships.

Perfectionism appears to result from a combination of innate tendencies and environmental influences. Some individuals seem to be inclined toward perfectionism at a very young age, and these tendencies can be exacerbated by how adults respond to them.

Perfectionist tendencies can be manifested in procrastination, thoroughness, social difficulties and overt perfectionism.

Procrastination:

This is putting off tasks for fear of not being able to complete them perfectly or not completing tasks because there is always room for improvement. To help a child counteract severe procrastination, parents can choose from the following activities:

- Encourage the child to change his/her goal from perfection to completion of tasks.
- Help the child break down tasks into manageable parts.
- Help the child develop realistic schedules.
- Teach the child to concentrate on tasks for several short time periods.
- Help the child prioritize and distinguish essential from non-essential details.

Thoroughness:

This is the difficulty of differentiating the important from the unimportant, and the excessive inclusion of detail in oral and written work. The tendency toward excessive physical clutter due to fear of discarding a potentially useful item can also be due to thoroughness. Some ways that parents can help the child are:

- Set one or two goals at the beginning of a project and help maintain focus on these goals.
- Work from outlines.
- Reduce clutter by asking whether or how often items have actually been needed, or having two steps to discarding (such as putting potentially discardable items into a box to be reviewed and discard after a time period).
- Help the child decide how much time to spend on a task and stick to a timetable.

Social Difficulties:

This can manifest itself as social inhibition due to fear of others seeing flaws, the need to be correct at all times, the inability to let others react emotionally, the tendency to criticize others, and the avoidance of social and romantic encounters. Here are some ways you can help:

- Encourage your child to become more aware of lack of others' perfection. For example, if your child is inhibited in beginning to speak a foreign language, have them take note of the lack of proficiency of the other students.
- Take gradual steps in attending social situations and joining groups.
- Model and encourage saying "I don't know."

- Model and encourage admitting errors without explaining self.
- Ask the child to focus on a positive quality in the person he is criticizing.
- Avoid comparing one child with another.

<u>Overt Perfectionism:</u>

Here is the belief that all tasks must be done perfectly and that perfection is a reasonable and desirable goal. To help a child counteract excessive perfectionism, parents can choose from the following activities:

- Encourage the child to prioritize and decide which activities deserve maximum energy and which activities are less important. Teach the child not to expect to perform equally well in all tasks.
- Model and encourage savoring success.
- Model and encourage relaxation such as meditation, listening to soothing music, yoga, cooking, etc.
- Set reasonable standards for yourself and for the child.
- "Fair pair"—make sure that every time a child is criticized, she/he is praised.
- Praise for accomplishments that have nothing to do with achievement, e.g. cooperation, sharing, remembering, playing well together, etc.
- Model and encourage saying "no" to requests that would overextend resources.

You may need to accept that you may never fully eradicate your child's perfectionism, but you can help him/her to deal with it. Let children know that while it's wonderful to begin with a grand vision, it's also all right if the end result is different from the original plan. Stress the importance of enjoying the process of whatever activity you are doing.

The ambitions of the perfectionist child are often greater than their current abilities, and it's difficult for these children to value where they are right now. Explain that the finished products will improve over time as the child gets more and more practice.

Especially with children who strive for perfection, it is important to help them understand that at times you simply have to accept "good enough." There is a fine line between trying to explain to a child the importance of getting things done in a timely manner and squashing their impulse to produce a quality result. If we don't strike a balance, we risk fostering an attitude that it's all right to turn in sloppy work.

Helping a child who suffers from perfectionism is a lifelong pursuit. Try not to give up and don't feel badly if you don't see immediate results. The goal of bringing awareness of finding the balance between their goals and what is realistic is an important life lesson that is worth pursuing on a continual basis for this child.

Here are a few other suggestions that you might consider:

- Have frequent adult/child conferences and self-evaluations to review areas of strength and successful accomplishments.
- Temper the child's tendency toward negative self-appraisal when performance did not meet unrealistic standards.
- Reinforce progress toward goals.

- Discuss your own strengths and weaknesses and emphasize that no one is superior in all areas.
- Model and encourage graceful acceptance of your own mistakes.
- Encourage becoming comfortable with uncertainty and ambiguity.
- Encourage the child to spend energy learning to care about and help others.
- Redefine the word "mistake"—think of mistakes as proof of learning and growing instead of failure.
- Discuss the benefits of making mistakes—stimulation of curiosity, creative energies, investigative skills, and adding to their knowledge of useful experiences.
- Have the student sign a contract to NOT be perfect; get a B, sleep late, etc.
- Discuss the lives of people who initially failed but later had success: Babe Ruth, Louisa May Alcott, Walt Disney, Thomas Edison, Abraham Lincoln, Albert Einstein, Benjamin Franklin, the Wright Brothers, Leonardo DaVinci, etc.
- Have the child list the advantages and disadvantages of perfectionism.
- Have the child keep a journal to log what happens before and after instances of perfectionism.
- Help the student determine what comments she/he is making to herself/himself that are critical, judgmental, and/or derogatory. Help them to develop alternative, more positive internal comments.
- Make sure the child knows that any grade other than an A is not a failure.
- Encourage self-compassion.

In summary, realistic self-expectations need to be carefully developed in children who suffer from perfectionism. Parental assistance can be a positive force to help this tendency to be moderated so that it can become an asset rather than a detriment.

Praise

Most of us have grown up believing that praise is desperately needed by all children in order to stimulate them into "right" behavior. If we watch a child closely when he/she is receiving praise we may discover some astonishing facts. Some children gloat, some panic, some express "so what?" and some seem to say, "Well, finally!"

We are suddenly confronted with the fact that we need to see how the child interprets what is going on rather than assume that he/she regards everything as we do.

Examination of the intention of the "praiser" shows that he is offering a reward. "If you are good you will have the reward of being held high in my esteem." Well fine. What is wrong with this approach? Why not help the child learn to do the right thing by earning a high place in parental esteem?

If we look at this situation from the child's point of view, we will find the mistake of this approach.

How does praise affect the child's self-image? He/she may get the impression that his/her personal worth depends upon how he/she "measures up" to the demands and values of others. "If I am praised, my personal worth is high. If I am scolded, I am worthless." When this child becomes an adult his/her effectiveness, his/her ability to function, and his/her capacity to cope with life's tasks will depend upon his/her estimation of how he/she stands in the opinion of others. He/she will live constantly on an elevator—up and down.

Praise is apt to center the attention of the child upon himself/herself. "How do I measure up?" rather than "What does this situation need?" This gives rise to a fictitious goal of "self being praised" instead of the reality goal of "What can I do to help?"

Another child may come to see praise as his/her right—as rightfully due to him/her from life. Therefore, life is unfair if he/she doesn't receive praise for every effort. "Poor me—no one appreciates me." Or, he/she may feel he/she has no obligation to perform if no praise is forthcoming. "What's in it for me? What will I get out of it? If no praise (reward) is forthcoming, why should I bother?"

Praise can be terribly discouraging. If the child's effort fails to bring the expected praise he/she may assume either that he/she isn't good enough or what he/she has to offer isn't worth the effort and give up.

If a child has set exceedingly high standards for himself/herself, praise may sound like mockery or scorn, especially when his/her efforts fail to measure up to his/her own standards. In such a child, praise only serves to increase his/her anger with himself/herself and his/her resentment towards others for not understanding his/her dilemma.

In all our efforts to encourage children we must be alert to the child's response. The accent must move from "What am I?" (good?) to "How can I help in the total situation?" Anything we do that reinforces a child's false image of himself/herself is discouraging. Whatever we do that helps a child see that he/she is part of a functioning unit that he/she can contribute to, cooperate with, and participate in is encouragement. We must learn to see that <u>as he/she is</u>, the child is good enough.

Praise rewards the <u>*individual*</u> and tends to fasten his/her attention upon himself. Little satisfaction or self-fulfillment comes from this direction.

Encouragement stimulates the effort and fastens attention upon one's capacity to join humanity and to become aware of interior strength and native capacity to cope.

Praise recognizes the actor, encouragement acknowledges the act.

Praise	Encouragement
Aren't you wonderful to be able to do this?	Isn't it nice that you can help?
	We appreciate your help.
	Don't the dishes shine? (after wiping)
	Isn't the carpet pretty now? (after vacuuming
	How nice your room looks!
	Thanks for watching the baby. It was a big help.
	I like your drawing. The colors are so pretty together.
	How much neater the room looks now that your toys are put away.
I'm so proud of you for getting good grades. (You are high in my esteem.)	I'm so glad you enjoy learning (adding to your own resources).

I'm proud of you for behaving so nicely in the restaurant.	We all enjoyed being together in the restaurant.
I'm awfully proud of your performance in the recital.	It is good to see that you enjoy playing. We all appreciate the job you did. I give you credit for working hard.

Many people do not know how or when to give appropriate and sincere praise and encouragement. Perhaps they received little praise when they were young and the words seem awkward and artificial, or they don't know what behaviors to praise.

Often parents who don't praise their children don't praise themselves either. If they listened to their internal "self-talk," they wouldn't hear things like "You're doing a good job of disciplining Johnny" or "You handled that conflict calmly and rationally." Instead they are quick to criticize themselves.

Those who are not in the habit of positive "self-talk" (or are too much in the habit of self-criticism) can learn to praise themselves. Then they will be more likely to do the same for their children. Praise and encouragement can have a dramatic impact on children's behavior. Here are some guidelines.

Be Specific: Specific or "labeled" praise describes the behavior you like. Instead of saying "Good job," you would say, "I'm pleased that you are remembering to feed the dog every day," or "I've noticed that you are making fewer spelling errors in your homework assignments."

<u>Show Enthusiasm</u>: Smile, make eye contact, give a pat on the back. Praise should be stated with energy and sincerity; words thrown carelessly over the shoulder will be lost on the child.

Caution: If giving praise feels difficult or you are not used to it, it may sound phony or boring initially. That's to be expected. Genuine positive feelings will come as you use praise more often. Here are a few phrases to help you get started:

- I like it when you...
- It really pleases me when you...
- You're doing just what I asked you to do.
- Hey, you are really sharp, you...
- I'm very proud of you for...
- Thank you for...
- That's a perfect way of...
- Wow, what a wonderful job you've done of...

<u>Praise Immediately</u>: While delayed praise is better than none, the most effective praise is given within five seconds of the positive behavior. If you're trying to encourage a new behavior, watch for every time it starts to happen. Don't wait for the clothes to be put on perfectly or the toys to all be put away. Praise your children as soon as they begin the desired behavior. The praise should be frequent and consistent in the beginning, then gradually become more intermittent.

<u>Don't Combine Praise with Commands or Criticism</u>: Without realizing it, some people undermine praise by combining it with a command (or a criticism!). A parent might say,

"You came to the table the first time I asked. That's great. But from now on, how about washing your face and hands first?" Or perhaps, "I'm glad you're making your bed, but why didn't you do it yesterday?" Praise should be clear and unequivocal, without reminders of prior failures or requests for future performance.

Reinforcing a new behavior is a long and difficult task. Whether you're using attention, a hug, a smile, or verbal praise, try to reinforce the positive behavior every time it occurs. If there are two adults in your family, discuss which behavior you want to improve and how you will try to reinforce it. With both participating, the learning will occur more quickly. In addition, adults can double the impact by praising children in front of other adults.

Praise should be a <u>sincere</u> result of a child doing something special, i.e. working toward a goal. It is important to always praise the effort as much as the result. Working hard to achieve a goal is worthy of praise.

Things to praise: cooperation in family and school, working together as a team, and one's role on the team.

However, it is important that children experience joy in many ways, but disappointment as well.

Parents need to model that a happy life always includes disappointment, mistakes, obstacles, pain, loss, and suffering in addition to "the good stuff."

<u>Words that Give Sincere Praise:</u>

That's incredible!
How extraordinary!
Outstanding performance!
Amazing effort!

Cool!
Excellent!
You are special!
Your project is first rate!
Thumbs up!
You are a good friend!
You tried hard!
You made it happen!
Bravo!
You set a great example for others!
The time you put in really shows!
Fine imagination!
Well done!
You figured it out!
Thanks for being honest!
How thoughtful of you!
You're getting there...keep trying!
What a great idea!
You're getting better...keep it up!
You can be trusted!
You really are growing up!
Great listener!
Thanks for caring!
Great discovery!
How original!

Self-Discipline/ Self-Control

Self-Discipline:

Self-discipline is the ability to set a realistic goal or make a plan—and then stick with it. It is the ability to resist doing things that can hurt others or ourselves. It involves keeping promises and following through on commitments. It is the foundation of many other qualities of character.

Often self-discipline requires persistence and sticking to long-term commitments—putting off immediate pleasure for later fulfillment. It also includes dealing effectively with emotions, such as anger and envy, and developing patience.

Learning self-discipline helps children regulate their behavior and gives them the willpower to make good decisions and choices. On the other hand, the failure to develop self-discipline leaves children wide open to destructive behavior. Without the ability to control or evaluate their impulses, they often dive headlong into harmful situations.

What To Do

- Talk with your child about setting reachable goals. For example, help him/her break big tasks into little tasks that can be accomplished one at a time. Have the child pick a task and set a deadline for completing it. When the deadline has passed, check together to see if the task was completed.

- Help your child build a sense of his/her competence. To do this, he/she needs experiences of success, no matter how small. This builds confidence and effort for the next time. Keep making the tasks just a little more challenging but doable.

"Who just called?

"It was my friend, Harry, Dad. He wanted me to go with him to check out new DVDs."

"What did you tell him?"

"I said I couldn't because you and I need to work on my science project for school."

Self-Control:

In the early years, parents are in control of much of what their children do—what they eat, what they do, where they go, etc. As children grow, though, we need to step back and relax our control, and instead help them to make good, independent decisions and resist impulses. Teaching self-control is an important piece and a vital skill in preparing children for life. Here are some steps you can take to help your children with self-control:

- Be a good role model and teach self-talk. Walk your children through your own decision-making process, thereby helping them to think before they act.
- Practice consistent parenting concerning limit-setting in your house. Both you and your partner/

spouse need to be in charge and stand united in your decisions—neither wavering. If a child feels he can get something by playing Mom against Dad, he/she will.

- Give your school-aged child more choices and freedom, allowing him/her to exercise self-control and to practice daily-life skills.
- Give your child an allowance and the ability to earn some money so that they can begin to take charge of their own spending and have some control over their own purchases.

It is important for each child's growth and development to have, at the appropriate time, some control and independence in their lives. By starting small and building on the positive, they will develop the self-control that will serve them well in the future.

SELF-ESTEEM/SELF-DOUBT

Self-esteem is having a positive attitude about ourselves. It is recognizing one's ability to learn and achieve. It is relating to others with positive feedback and reaching one's fullest potential.

Encouragement from parents and teachers is essential for children to grow in self-esteem. Children need to be told they are special, and, through their hard work and effort, begin to see that, indeed, they are special. As children feel positive about what they can do academically, creatively, socially, and physically, their self-esteem continues to build throughout the years.

Children with good self-esteem do not want to hurt others by teasing or bullying. They recognize that calling people names, talking behind someone's back, taking someone else's things, and hitting or pushing someone around hurts their feelings and body and makes them feel unhappy, afraid, and angry. Hurting or upsetting someone creates feelings of unhappiness that are difficult to heal.

At School

One of the most hurtful things elementary-age children respond to is exclusion. To not be included in a play group or activity, from a birthday party to play dates to playing a game at recess on the playground or not being chosen to be on a team, are very damaging to a child's self-esteem.

Therefore, as meaningful adults in children's lives, it is most important to keep encouraging them to try hard to do their best at what they learn. Equally important is to be vigilant about how children are responding in group activities where teasing and bullying can fester and lead to exclusion, resulting in unhappiness and poor self-esteem. The need to feel accepted by adults, as well as by peer groups, is an important ingredient for developing positive self-esteem.

All parents want their children to feel good about themselves. There are many school activities that children engage in that encourage and bolster healthy self concepts. However, the primary input comes from parents who show love, respect, and acceptance for them. Praise is most important, but children need to know that the most genuine praise comes from hard work and striving to meet realistic expectations based upon age and ability.

Children need to be able to face challenges that will motivate them to do better, receive praise, and feel good about their own effort to achieve a goal.

For years, people have wondered why some individuals are go-getters and take pride in their work, and, on the other hand, why some are not motivated to reach their fullest potential. The go-getters are usually people with lots of self-confidence. They have good self-esteem and a positive attitude about themselves. They enter into situations expecting to win. And how did they learn to have this positive attitude? The answer is through encouragement from others. They were told they were special. They learned how to learn and master the skills that directly affect their self-concept.

At times parents need to look hard for opportunities to praise their child. They need to focus in on the appropriate things the child does. Tell him/her what it is that he/she is doing that we like. If he/she knows what it is we like, he/she is likely to do it again. It is normal for children to want to please adults, especially their parents, during the elementary school ages (five to twelve).

To make sure that self-esteem is genuine and everlasting, the following are ways to accomplish this:

Use of Praise

Do not use praise just to make your child feel good. Make it meaningful by praising only accomplishments that require real effort.

Use Proactive Feedback

Be specific (i.e. "You really know how to sound out words with short a" or "You know your multiplication tables through nine" or "You really know how to write a good paragraph") and then tell them how pleased you are.

Mistakes are Normal

Help your children to look at and admit their mistakes. The only meaningful learning comes about by trial and error. It is important to legitimize their mistakes and ability to take risks. Be a good model in this area.

Gift Giving

Save gift giving for birthdays and holidays. This will make it very special. Do not lavish gifts because "everyone has a specific toy or dress" and your child need not compete with peers. "In our family we give gifts only on special occasions."

Grades are important but not stressful

Children need to know their progress reports are important, but that you do not base love and approval upon a "good progress report." If your child is having difficulty learning, being angry or punitive will not help. Children need to know that parents want to help, not criticize. A more relaxed and supportive attitude at home will go a long way toward giving them a solid sense of self-esteem. If the situation requires professional help, provide it for your child so he/she feels your support.

Encourage Challenges

Children gain self-esteem by taking on work that pushes them to the limits of their skills. Success will encourage them to develop good self-esteem and accept new challenges. "Trying to do one's best" should be a slogan in every family.

Self-Esteem and Bullying

Most bullies have low self-esteem and they are angry, scared, lonely, and afraid that others will not like them. In truth, they do not like themselves and show it by hurting and insulting others. They tend to be jealous of other people's accomplishments. They can become frustrated because they don't feel they are good at anything. They rely on the skill they do have, scaring others. Children who feel excluded from family and school activities feel isolated and alone. It is most important to give your child opportunities to earn acceptance by structuring activities that can be done at home (i.e. chores, special privileges for placement in family, and rewards for accomplishment). The acceptance of your children as being special and deserving is essential to developing self-esteem.

Happiness vs. Indulgence
It is said that a happy family is usually a productive family. This is not always true. For instance, we need to be aware that permissiveness does not create happiness, satisfaction, or good relationships in a family. It usually leads to demanding behavior, lack of drive, and poor values. Indulgences and permissiveness have the same results of low expectations. Parents who lead a happy family have high expectations for performance at home and at school and help stretch children to meet those standards. Low expectations will not help achieve happiness, good relationships, and healthy self-esteem. Children derive security from a family where there are expectations, organization, consistency, and cause and effect for behavior. Rewards/praise for effort expended on a child's part are significant ingredients for self-esteem.

Help Your Child Bounce Back From Self-Doubt

Even the most positive children go through stages of self-doubt. Their self-esteem plummets because of a bad grade. Or they compare themselves to others and see themselves coming up short.

You know your child is going through one of these stages when you hear him/her say things like, "I can't do it!" "I'm no good at science" or "Maria hates me!"

You Can Help Your Child Bounce Back and Feel More Capable By:

- Laying the foundation for optimism. Break down difficult tasks into small steps your child can master. Let your child see that one success can lead to another.

- Teaching problem-solving skills. Brainstorm possible solutions. Give your child choices.
- Criticizing actions, not your child. "You didn't pick up your dirty clothes." Not, "You're lazy and messy." The latter implies there's something wrong with his/her character.
- Role playing your child's worries. If your child is afraid of making a new friend, let him/her practice introducing himself/herself to you.
- Talking about positive thinking on a regular basis. Point out positive versus negative attitudes from news or life stories. Share positive quotes from famous people.
- If your child expresses fears about the world, terrorism, etc., reassure him/her that as parents you are taking every precaution to help keep your child and the family safe.

Sibling Rivalry

A parent asked this question: "My 8 year old son and 5 year old daughter are constantly fighting and arguing. Needing to decide who is right and who to punish is driving me to distraction. How can I handle this issue? "

My answer: You are describing a most common problem that has not changed over the years and certainly will not be changed by this technological age we are living in. It is known as *sibling rivalry.* Often children present rivalrous behaviors not because they are angry or frustrated with each other, but for the benefit of the parent. Attention getting on the part of children can be a strong need, strong enough to receive negative attention from a parent. Attention is attention, whether it be good or bad– if you need it.

If you can't ignore the problem, which no doubt is hard to do, then discipline both children's behavior. It is not important who started it or who hit whom. The important action is to terminate the behavior. This is not by talk, but by sending both children to their rooms (or separate rooms) to stay until you are ready to ask them to come out.

It doesn't help to explain to the older one that, because he/she is older, you expect he/she will understand and give in to baby sister. This only tends to infuriate children and increase their dislike for the sibling.

So tell them both, if this bickering or fighting continues, they both will be sent to their rooms to think about it, and there will be no talk about how it started or who said a word to whom.

Talk or explain to children only when they are calm and ready to listen. Nothing is accomplished if you attempt to talk with them when they are upset, angry or frustrated.

You might also add a chart for each child and reward them each day for arguments or disagreements they settle without fighting. At the end of the week, a special reward can be earned for their good effort. If getting your attention is at the root of this problem, you need to find special time to be with each child alone so each can feel very important, a most basic need for emotional growth.

Special Time at Home

When children seem to need more attention, parents often say, "But we spent all day or weekend with him/her." We need to realize that time alone is not enough because we may have been distracted during the time we spent. Perhaps we were pulled away to talk on the phone, answer the door, chat with a neighbor, wash dishes, or do chores. Whatever the distraction, we took our attention away from our child.

The difference between special time and "time spent all day" is that special time is *quality* time and "time spent all day" is simply a *quantity* of time. Of course, parents cannot stop the routine of their workdays, so it is important to structure time with children, much as you would plan and structure anything else. When a child knows that he/she will spend half an hour or more with you several times a week without interruption, he/she will feel listened to and attended to more deeply than if he/she was just hanging around the house or going shopping with you all day.

Special time can be therapeutic for your children—a time when he/she feels unique, fulfilled, and heard. When children are given time alone with their parents, they feel that their needs have been met, no matter the activity. You could be eating a dinner together at a special restaurant, taking a walk in the park, playing a favorite game, watching a movie, reading aloud together, or just talking and communicating feelings that might otherwise have been unexpressed. No matter what you choose, your undivided attention will make your child feel special and important. Consistency is necessary since your child will look forward to these moments alone with you, sharing something enjoyable with the most valuable person in the world to them.

This sounds so simple, but it isn't. To have it really work, parents need to learn what it is to focus on a child with complete attention, so that the child feels really heard. This entails what we call *good active listening*. If you want your child to really talk with you and open up, then you must focus on their feelings and not just what they are saying. This is the time for a child to express their thoughts with someone he/she knows is listening, and who is not telling them what to do or how to feel. Children can be remarkably refreshed by such an experience, and parents get to know their child in ways that usually don't happen in the ordinary day to day of life.

This is a process that takes time to build. By consistently having daily special time, or at a minimum once a week, children will learn to eventually develop the trust to communicate their true feelings and needs with you. As a parent, it just doesn't get any better than that!

Styles of Parenting

There are three basic styles of Parenting:

- Authoritarian
- Permissive
- Authoritative

Authoritarian Parents
Have a lot of demands and give threats with little reassurance
Low in nurturing or acceptance
High on structure and firmness
Low on support for autonomy

Permissive Parents
High on affection but low on authority
Easygoing, highly accepting and nurturing
Low in control and tolerate a lot of autonomy
Soft and indulgent (wants child to be "happy")
Tend to have a peer-like relationship with the child. The result is that the children are self-centered and not tuned into the needs and wishes of others.
Often lack a sense of duty and conscience to expect things to go their way without having to work hard
Tend to be disengaged and disconnected with their child's life

Authoritative Parents

High on authority, reasoning, fairness and love

Explain reasons behind demands

Encourage give and take

Set standards and enforce them firmly, but does not regard self as infallible

Foster academic and social competency, empathy, consideration towards others, self-esteem and the ability to self-regulate

Present optimistic and perseverance messages to children

Research finds that at all age levels, the most confident and socially responsible children have authoritative parents. Parents need to exercise their right to be respected and obeyed, but do so through reasoning, fairness, and love. Disrespectful speech or behavior on the part of the child should not be tolerated. This clear understanding of behavior will then be transferred to teachers and school.

Take Time for Reflection

Parenting is the hardest job there is, and one in which we get no training. It can be easy to become so ingrained in the everyday stresses of work and of caring for children that we can lose sight of their growth and developmental successes, failures, hurts, and bruises. Therefore, we need time when we are away from them to reflect on what we are doing to internalize our values, behavior, experiences, etc. Introspective parents continually look within themselves in their action toward their children and the family as a whole.

It is the ability and willingness to reflect that makes the difference between simply functioning in daily routine life activities and making thoughtful decisions. The question parents need to be asking themselves is: How can we become <u>more</u> introspective with our children and our family as a whole?

There are a few significant things you can do to make reflection a critical factor in your everyday life:

1. Find or create regular periods of quiet time to delve inside yourself and reconnect with who you really are. Where and how long you choose to reflect is up to you. It can be a few minutes in the morning or an hour before you go to bed. But, it is necessary for your mental health and effectiveness as a parent to start a reflection. Everyone's mind needs refueling on a constant basis.

2. Another strategy is to start a reflective journal that you can use as if you were writing to a trusted friend. There is something about putting thoughts on paper, having to organize them into sentences and paragraphs, which clarifies your thinking and creates a sense of closure on issues you may be pondering.

Don't forget to take care of yourself and give yourself the time to recharge so that parenting can be a source of enjoyment and satisfaction to you as well as your children.

TEACHABLE MOMENTS

It is important to make teachable moments a part of every family's life. By taking advantage of "moments" we can model appropriate behavior and create a sense of right and wrong for our children. Children learn best through modeling adult behavior.

An everyday occurrence, like finding something of value and delivering it to its rightful owner, is an act of kindness for a neighbor. Encourage your child to make an extra effort to be kind to a friend who is lonely, or visit a food pantry. If we become aware of those in the environment around us, there is always a person in need of a helping hand, food, care, etc. These tasks are small but can have a huge impact on your child's way of looking at life. These are the moments when children truly learn the lessons of kindness and compassion that can make a deep impression on their minds.

Parents can practice teachable moments on a daily basis. These moments can happen anywhere—market, ball field, walking in a shopping mall, or even setting the table for dinner. Example—a most common teachable moment happens every time you drive your car with your children inside. Start with putting on your seat belt, to teach about about personal responsibility; or you might let someone into your lane on the freeway to teach about mutual respect for others and doing your part to help avoid accidents; stop at a stop sign to teach about the importance of obeying stop signs; you could put money into someone's parking meter that is showing expired, a lesson in helping another person not get a ticket. Of course, taking your child to a homeless shelter with an offering of clothes is also a teachable moment.

Children often learn moral lessons unconsciously in casual moments.

- Be aware of situations that represent moral choices.
- Praise your children for ethical choices.
- Point out ethical behavior in others.
- Let your children see your thought processes regarding ethical decisions.

Children need to learn early in their development that these are the skills that will guide them through adulthood and will give them understanding of and empathy for others along the way. It is never too early to begin to model the many teachable moments in everyday life.

TEACHING RESPONSIBILITY AT HOME

Talk with your children about the chores they find interesting and fun, and those they find boring and disagreeable. Perhaps make a list of jobs they'd like to try and jobs they want to avoid.

The results could surprise you. The jobs your children like might be harder and more time consuming than the ones they hate. Why? It might be because the jobs are more interesting or challenging. Maybe they involve real adult responsibilities. Children can feel that same pride and self-confidence we get from doing satisfying work.

Now look at the jobs your children hate. Are they ones like picking up dirty clothes, weeding the garden, making the bed, or taking out the garbage? These are the jobs many parents assign children, and children dislike them for the same reasons we do: They're boring! Dull jobs are a part of life too, but they can be made more appealing.

Ways to Make Boring Jobs More Appealing:

- Tell your children you need—and appreciate—their help. If they know you're counting on them, chances are they'll take their responsibilities more seriously.

- Work out a rotation system so each person also gets to do the more interesting tasks.
- Keep in mind that children don't always have the time for chores. Make your system flexible enough to work around sport practices, music lessons, and so on. Try to decide if some chores can be done less frequently or even eliminated.
- For younger children, break jobs into smaller steps so they're easier. For example, making a bed can be frustrating for young children. Showing them how to pull the bed out from the wall, make neat corners, and so on will make the job easier and more pleasant.
- Point out the positive results of your children's actions. "Bring your laundry down so you'll have clean clothes for tomorrow." "If we all do the housework together on Saturday morning, we'll have time to go swimming in the afternoon."
- Remember to notice and praise your children when they do their jobs, even if they do them only occasionally at first. Appreciation is the best encouragement.

For your children, being more responsible will mean accomplishing more things on their own. That's great, but they still depend on us for other things. At this time in their lives, we adults need to be a rock of support, listening to them and taking care of them when they need us.

To help your children become more responsible, give them interesting, challenging tasks (along with the dull ones), and support their efforts to accomplish them. Give less criticism and direction. Praise them for doing their very best even if it is not perfect. As they become more capable and skilled, let them take charge of increasingly more important tasks.

Responsibilities give students the internal motivation to behave appropriately.

Test Anxiety and Tips

Reducing Test Anxiety

Some students suffer from "test anxiety." They worry so much about the test that they worry themselves into a poor performance. Here are some things you can tell your child to help soothe the nerves:

- There are specific skills involved in taking tests that others have learned—and your child can learn them too. Some people are naturally good at basketball, while others need to learn the skills. The same is true about taking tests. If you don't have test-taking skills, don't worry. You can learn them.
- Good test scores aren't everything. Make sure your child knows how important attendance, attitude, homework, and daily class participation are. Test scores are just part of the grade.
- One test score—high or low—is just one test score. If most of your child's grades show he/she understands a subject, one low test score won't be a disaster.
- Make sure your child knows you love him/her no matter what. He/she should know that you expect him/her to do his/her best—but that doesn't mean he/she has to be the best on every test. No matter what the test grades, you are there to support him/her if they truly tried.

Test Taking Tips

- Remind your child to listen to and follow directions. Before giving a test, teachers tell students things they need to know—and that can be the difference between a high or a low score. Should students try to guess if they're not sure of an answer? Should the essay question be three or five good paragraphs? Does each paragraph need a topic sentence? Make sure your child listens to what the teacher has to say.
- Give your child practice in following directions. Make a game of it. Give your child a recipe and ask him/her to follow it. Or ask your child to look through a newspaper article and circle all the nouns, verbs, or adjectives. Try timing your children as they complete these tasks—tests often have a time limit.
- Make sure your child is physically ready to take the test. Aside from studying, the next best preparation is a good night's sleep before the test. Make sure he/she eats a good breakfast. Encourage him/her to wear a sweater than can be removed—there's nothing worse than being too hot or too cold.

The Importance of Organization

Things to Organize

It's easier for children to organize schoolwork and homework if other parts of life are organized, too, including:

- Belongings

Make sure your child has specific places to keep his things. You'll be less likely to hear, "Mom, where is my favorite shirt?" Or, "I can't find my house key!"

- TV/Computer time

Preferably, children should not watch TV or be on the computer on school days (M–Th). Weekdays should be limited to approximately 5 hours or less. To limit viewing, help your child plan which shows to watch. If special programs come on a week day, tape them for later viewing.

- Chores.

There's nothing wrong with expecting kids to help around the house. Make a chart explaining chores and when they should be done. As jobs are completed, kids can check them off.

- Daily routines.

Your child should be able to count on doing some things regularly. For example, eating breakfast before school, having dinner as a family, laying clothes out before bed or going to bed at a certain time.

- Extracurricular activities:

Encourage your child to participate in after-school activities he likes. But if they conflict with school work or family time, he'll have to cut back.

The Importance of Play

Play is a child's "job." Unfortunately, between television, computers, and scheduled activities, children are left with very little time in which to do their job. Playing provides great learning opportunities and also gives children some much needed time to simply be children. Playing also helps children develop their imaginations and build motor and social skills. Here are some great tips to help get your children playing.

Limit TV. Children spend too much time in front of the television and computer. Limiting access will encourage them to engage in other activities. If they need or enjoy the background noise, turn on the radio. Music will entice your children to sing, dance, and use their imaginations.

Don't rush. Just like adults, children need time to unwind and time for their imaginations to start working. Try to provide daily time for unstructured and unscheduled play; time when your children can decide what, when, and how to play.

Be creative. Children don't need the latest, greatest toys. All you really need are a few basic essentials such as crayons, dress-up clothes, books, and balls. Keep "open-ended" materials around—things that children can use for more than one type of play, from modeling clay to old sheets to wooden blocks to cardboard boxes.

Don't believe the hype. Many educational toys tout benefits you might never see. Before you spend a lot of money on educational toys or electronics, ask your child's teacher for recommendations. While the electronic globe looks great and has a lot of features, puzzles or a craft kit might better serve your child's needs. Involve your child in the discussion and purchase of toys. You want to make sure you choose toys with which they will actually play.

Run around. Regardless of whether or not your child plays organized sports, make time several days a week for them to run around and exercise. From swinging a bat to swinging on a swing set, physical activity helps kids grow strong and release some energy.

Play games. When children play games, they learn important social lessons. Team games help teach skills such as how to work together, how to handle conflict, and how to strategize. Board games teach skills such as sharing, taking turns, and the art of compromise. Playing games also teaches children how to be graceful winners and good losers. While parents and caregivers can be game "partners," it's more important to have children interact with siblings or peers.

Expect play. After-school and summer childcare programs can be wonderful opportunities for children to play—or they can be play busters. When looking at these programs, ask how much time your child will have to play and how much time is spent watching TV and playing computer or video games. Choose a program you feel allows your child enough time to play and use his or her imagination.

The most important thing is to allow your children to be children and learn through play.

UNDERSTANDING COURAGE

Is it OK to talk about our feelings in our family? Do we talk about others' feelings?

Courage is the ability to recognize and refrain from a negative action such as teasing. Courage means doing the right thing, and speaking out on behalf of others when necessary. It takes courage to stand up and "call others off" for teasing. It takes courage and strength of character to "bite your tongue" at your first reaction. It takes courage to apologize for something that hurt another person.

Courage in Action

You can foster courage in your child as he/she faces the problem of teasing by helping him/her to:

- Recognize when to refrain from and when to stand up to peer pressure.
- Recognize that when he/she is uncomfortable with teasing, the situation has probably gone too far, and that he/she needs to have the courage to resist it.
- Create boundaries by saying, "In our house, teasing is not allowed."
- Discover what he/she has in common with peers—they are less likely to tease someone they have gotten to know.

Family Courage Checklist

- Do we own up to mistakes in our family?
- Do we apologize when we have hurt or offended someone else?
- Do we talk about examples of courage in everyday life?
- Can we disagree in our house without being criticized?
- Do we support each other when someone has "gone out on a limb" and shown courage?

With common sense, back-to-basics suggestions from experienced parents, and the practical advice of scholars, teachers, and experts in character education, Full Circle strives to offer parents accessible approaches for thinking through the realities of raising their children with a focus on developing virtue.

Source: The Full Circle Family Foundation, reprinted in CHARACTER (newsletter for the Center for Advancement of Ethics and Character) Summer 2001

About Feeling Unique and Special

All children need and want to feel important and special. Some children are able to express this feeling easily to parents and teachers, while others may find it more difficult to let adults know how they feel and how important it is to receive reinforcement for who they are.

This Area of Specialness:

What makes every child special is his/her unique qualities, talents, and desires. At Laurence, your child's efforts to do his/her best in all areas of development—social, emotional, and academic—merit praise when truly earned and deserved. Receiving sincere praise is important for children to work toward as a goal, no matter what their age. When praising or recognizing good effort or accomplishments, you, the adult, are feeding your child's self-esteem.

At home, children need to be valued for their strengths, interests, talents, and relationships with others, whether they are the only-child or one of many in the family. You, the parent, can reinforce your child's efforts to develop his/her strengths in the many different ways, i.e. sports, music, drama, chess, science, academics etc.

Special Time at Home

When children seem to need more attention, parents often say, "But, we spend all day or weekend with him or her." We need to realize that time alone is not enough because we may have been distracted during the time we spent. Perhaps we were pulled away to talk on the telephone, answer the door, chat with our neighbors, wash dishes, or do chores. Whatever the distraction, we took our attention away from our child.

The difference between *special time* and "*time spent all day*" is that *special time is quality time* and "*time spent all day*" is simply a quantity of time. Of course, parents cannot stop the routine of their workdays, so it's important to structure time with children, much as you would plan and structure anything else. When a child knows that he/she will spend half an hour or more with you several times a week without interruption, he/she will feel listened and attended to more deeply than if he/she was just hanging around the house or going shopping with you all day.

Special Individualized Time

Special time can be therapeutic for your children—a time when he/she feels unique, fulfilled, and heard. When children are given time alone with their parents, they feel that their needs have been met, no matter the activity. You could be eating a dinner together at a special restaurant, taking a walk in the park, playing a favorite game, watching a movie, reading aloud together, or just talking and communicating feelings that might otherwise have been unexpressed. No matter what you chose, your undivided attention will make your child feel special and important. Consistency is necessary since your child will look forward to these moments alone with you, sharing something enjoyable with the most valuable person in the world.

This sounds so simple, but it isn't! To have it really work, parents need to learn what it is to focus on a child with complete attention, so that the child feels he/she is really being heard. This entails what we call *good active listening*. If you want your child to really talk with you and open up, you must focus on feelings and not "confuse" "stop" with "facts." This is the time for a child to express feelings with someone he/she knows is listening and not telling them what to do or feel. Children can be remarkably refreshed by such an experience, and parents get to know them in ways that usually don't happen in ordinary day-to-day living.

This is a process that takes time to build. By consistently having daily or a minimum of special time once a week, children will learn to eventually develop trust and communicate their true feelings and needs.

Appreciating Diverse Cultures Through Art

Chapter Four
Children

The teacher plays a pivotal role in educating the "Total Child," and their job involves more than having a body of knowledge.

For real learning to occur, the teacher must first establish relationships with each child, so that all feel safe, engaged, supported, and appropriately challenged. With these things in place, the benefits of formal, structured learning can be achieved. And the benefits are more than the tools for future learning or the accrual of skills by which one can earn a living.

Expectations of teachers are great here at the Laurence School, but students and teachers alike reap the benefits of understanding what I have discovered in the following section. These concepts give teachers insights into how to have a successful class and a more enjoyable and satisfying teaching experience. And most importantly, students are the ultimate beneficiaries of these approaches, which enable them to find purpose and pleasure in the classroom.

Working With Children and Parents

Knowing the children we teach—individually, culturally, and developmentally—is as important as knowing the content we teach.

Knowing the families of the children we teach and working with them as partners is essential to children's education.

How children learn is as important as what they learn; process and content go hand in hand.

To be successful academically and socially, children need a set of social skills, which includes cooperation, assertion, responsibility, empathy, and self-control.

The social curriculum is as important as the academic curriculum.

The greatest cognitive growth occurs through social interaction.

How the adults at school work together is as important as their individual competence; lasting change begins with the adult community.

Practice strategies for helping children build academic and social-emotional competencies day in and day out. In urban, suburban, and rural settings nationwide, educators using these strategies report increased student engagement and academic progress, along with fewer discipline problems.

Challenges for Educators in the Twenty-First Century

Laurence School stands firmly at the crossroads of the past, present, and future in educating children. Our students need to develop a high degree of mastery of basic academic skills, learn to be caring and giving to others, be proficient in the use of technology to open up vast horizons of information and connections, and be prepared to meet the challenges of the twenty-first century. They need to see their roles in contributing to this new world by studying about topics like global warming, transportation, waste management, healthcare, poverty, etc. Their understanding and knowledge of what they imagine they can do to contribute in these areas is important. Talents such as creativity, collaboration, communication, empathy, and adaptability are the core capabilities that will help children learn to live a more successful life. Therefore, we need to create an environment that raises lots of questions for children and then help them to translate this information into their own understanding. Real learning comes when children are able to question and truly seek out answers. Parents and teachers need to be the enablers of learning rather than the "experts" giving answers to questions.

Children's basic needs have continued to be constant over the past decades, including their need for:

- Physical and emotional safety in their ongoing development
- Physical development
- Love, respect, and attention from caring adults as caretakers and guides
- Happy and satisfying friendships
- Curiosity and brain stimulation from parents and teachers—mastery skills that affect self-esteem

Today's children, unlike those who grew up in generations past, have the advantage of technology, the Internet, and social networks that bring the world closer than we could ever have imagined. Our school believes in the value of these resources available to children that instill within them an even greater joy for learning and leads to thinking, discovering, and discussion. We need to identify opportunities for growth with courage and be open to new thinking that can be incorporated into the development of the "Total Child."

Although technology holds a very clear place in our children's futures, there is some cause for concern. Some of the areas that we see directly impacted by technology are deficits in the areas of empathy, concentration, and attention. Because these skills are so crucial for learning, we have to make sure that they can be provided in other ways. Another area of concern is in the art of conversation. We need to make sure that we don't lose face to face interactions with friends, family, and teachers, which can be a source of pleasure and can broaden perspectives and understanding between people. Actual conversations offer children the opportunity to relate and take in information, offer an opinion, and understand another human being. These skills offer children the chance for higher level thinking, as does the reading of an actual book. The glare of the e-reader and the motivation to finish and move on to something else deprives our children of the ability to stop, think about "what if," or analyze characters and encourage imagination.

Helping children to understand the importance of knowing the difference between appropriate and inappropriate information from these sources will continue to be an ongoing challenge for schools and homes. It is difficult to know and access what a child is taking in from this individual programming without some verbal interaction and/or discussion. It will require consistent monitoring of children's strong interest in the visual and immediate gratification through the media. The goal should be to create balance between reading and conversation among family members and the excitement of the offerings of the Internet that can be a solo activity.

We need to accept that today's children are part of a digital generation—the first group of students to see technology as a provider of their productivity tools. They do and will learn differently, and, consequently, we need to teach them differently. With information expanding at this rapid rate, it is no longer reasonable to ask children to memorize history, literature, and science, as was common practice in years past. As educators, we must focus our teaching on how to think, to access and to assess, to analyze, and to communicate well with others.

It is vital that every student who graduates from the sixth grade knows how to assemble and collate information and to draw conclusions from a vast variety of information.

Language arts, social studies, and math can no longer be taught in isolation. All disciplines must work together and be integrated to help students address issues that are authentic to the world in which they live, and teachers must, through the use of technology, direct children to problems that are true to the world in hopes that they will find the answers. Preparation for life issues is paramount. We will still teach "the basics," but in a different way.

We twenty-first century educators are responsible for teaching a new generation—one that is exposed to all kinds of new information. We must therefore take this as a challenge and an opportunity to explore new ways to reach children and different ways for them to learn. We must view change as an opportunity to look toward the future and provide children with the academic and social-emotional tools to be successful and happy in this ever-changing world.

Characteristics of a Successful Classroom:

- Students need to experience themselves as valued contributing and influential members of their classroom.
- There needs to be respectful, supportive relationships among students, teachers, and parents.
- Students are able to ask questions, give opinions, make mistakes, reflect on a new experience, try a new way to do an activity, and do all the risk-taking that true learning entails.
- There are frequent opportunities to help and collaborate with others.
- Information is taught, as often as possible, by doing.
- An emphasis on common purpose and ideals is essential.
- Empathy is fostered in each child so that all members of the class show concern and caring for the others in their class.

Compacts for Excellence

This is the concept that teachers and students are all in this together and that we will accomplish our goals by creating strategies and evaluating our progress along the way. The Compact for Excellence provides a pathway from *knowing* what is right to *doing* what is right.

Creating a compact at the beginning of the school year serves several purposes:

- It clearly communicates what our school/classroom values are: doing our best and being our best.
- It sends the message to students that while teachers have high expectations for students, they also have high expectations for themselves.

Teachers can use various methods to hold class members accountable to their compact.

- Some teachers assess regularly, asking students to rate, on a scale of zero to five, how well the class is doing on a particular item (e.g., "How well are we doing with not pushing to get to the front of the line?") Students each put a post-it with their rating next to that item.
- Some teachers pick a single item—one that is continually receiving the lowest score—to focus on for the entire week, and this item is assessed at the end of every day.

<u>Classroom Compact Example:</u>

To help everyone feel welcome, respected, and cared about:

Students will ...

- treat people the way they want to be treated
- be kind, respectful, and responsible toward everyone
- think before they act
- respect teachers and school property

- be cooperative and honest
- apologize (then everyone will forgive and forget)

The teacher will ...

- greet every student
- understand that each student is different
- treat everyone kindly

To help everyone do their best work:

Students will ...

- never settle for less than their best
- be inspired to learn
- listen carefully and raise their hands if they want to speak
- be quiet while others are working
- ask for help when they need it
- have a positive attitude and try to bounce back after disappointments

The teacher will ...

- prepare lessons well and do her best teaching
- give interesting homework
- call upon all students in class
- provide individual help

Compacts are an excellent way to insure a more successful classroom.

Guidelines for the "Intelligence-Friendly Classroom"

- Establish a safe emotional climate. In such a climate, risk-taking is the norm, and students feel that wrong answers are as much a part of learning as right answers. Specific strategies include tapping into the emotional intelligences of the learners and organizing diverse small-group work.
- Create a rich learning environment. Use presentations of science equipment, art supplies, or computers designed to stimulate curiosity. Create "mini-environments" that facilitate a variety of activities, including one-on-one interactions between students and between the teacher and the student, quiet reflection, and learning centers. Sensory input—music, print materials, visually appealing bulletin boards—can also engage students' interest.
- Teach the mind-tools and skills of life. These run the gamut from communication skills necessary in any social environment to skills needed to program computers. Specific skills might include critical thinking (prioritizing, comparing, and judging), creative thinking (inferring, predicting, and generalizing), social skills (team leadership and

conflict resolution), technological skills (keyboarding and searching the Internet), visual skills (painting and sculpting), and performance arts (dancing and acting).

- Develop the skillfulness of the learner. Student skills are developed through mediation, practice, coaching, and rehearsal. Skill development occurs through formal teaching structures—such as direct instruction—as well as through independent readings and research and the dialogue of peer coaching and mentoring.
- Challenge students with hands-on learning opportunities. These would include lab-like situations and other real-life experiences that invite the learner to become an integral part of the process.
- Involve many facets of intelligence. It is not necessary to include all eight intelligences in every lesson, but teachers might reasonably try to incorporate several different ways of understanding in any given assignment. For example, working on a classroom newspaper requires that students interview (interpersonal), write (verbal), design and lay out (visual), and critique (logical).
- Transfer learning from the public arena to the personal. Through reflection, make learning meaningful and relevant. Possible tools for reflection include reading-response journals, in which the reader writes a personal, immediate response to what has been read, and learning logs, which record thoughts, comments, and questions prior to or following an experience.
- Balance traditional assessment measures with portfolios and performance assessments. In addition to letter grades, use portfolio assessments (on collections of students' best work) and performance assessments (on speeches, presentations, plays, concerts, etc.).

Mindsets and Innovation

The term growth mindset was coined by Carol Dweck of Stanford University to explain why some individuals seem to succeed in almost anything they set their mind to. After conducting several powerful experiments and producing long-term studies, she found evidence of two mindsets:

In a fixed mindset, people believe their basic qualities, like their intelligence or talent, are simply fixed traits. They spend their time documenting their intelligence or talent instead of developing them. They also believe that talent alone creates success—without effort. They're wrong, according to Dweck.

There are varying degrees of growth and fixed mindsets—these mindsets describe two extremes of a spectrum. Also, we can have a growth mindset in one area (If I practice my volleyball serve for an hour every day, I will eventually ace it consistently), and have a fixed mindset in other areas (I can't draw. I'm no artist). But no matter the field or skill, the evidence is clear that a growth mindset can make the difference between success and failure.

I attribute my personal success in this area to my upbringing, even if my parents and teachers did not know the terminology at the time. I have taught the growth mindset to my sixth-grade science students and have seen a positive impact. Students are more willing to tackle challenges and seek feedback, and they bounce back from setbacks more easily.

In my six decades of work at Laurence, I learned that a growth mindset helps one learn from setbacks, and is the key to optimism. There are no failures as we move into the future with innovation. However, we need to view mindset as a journey that helps us to persist, especially when things don't turn out the way one would expect.

In order to grow, we have to seek and welcome feedback in the innovation process. As we learn to embrace new things and challenges, we find there are multiple ways to solve a problem successfully.

It is indeed our mission as educators to fulfill our mission to prepare students for a changing world.

Classroom Strategies Related to Academic Progress and Development/Mindsets

All students need to know that intelligence and/or living "smart" is not fixed. It is not connected with learning/achieving more than anything else. It is important that students know they have the power to develop their own intelligence through constant practice and seeking new challenges.

Here are some classroom strategies to support a growth mindset:

- Praise effort and choices of persistence, not just success
- Engage students in goal-setting
- Coach children to expect and get excited about challenging work
- Design homework tasks that stretch learning to novel applications or the next level
- Think about how grading can evolve to recognize persistent effort and growth over time

The classroom must recognize hard work and not just the "right answers." We need to encourage children to dream and give them the tools to work toward those dreams.

CREATIVITY CAN BE TAUGHT

Success in the modern world demands innovation, complex problem solving, and new ways of understanding; it requires creativity.

Creativity is often thought of as it applies to the areas of the arts—music, dance, visual arts, writing, etc. However, in addition to these important talents, it is vital that creativity is also integrated into all academic, social, and emotional areas of development. It encourages children to think of new ways of looking at and solving problems, and to understand things in a novel way. It allows children to think about what is stated, to offer opinions, and to back up their opinion in a "creative "way.

As children begin to think deeply about any subject or social issue, they learn the importance of sometimes thinking "outside the box." This is an essential ability and lifelong skill.

Teachers can play an important role in encouraging all children to think creatively about problems or issues that require more than a yes or no answer. It opens up the possibility that there is more than one way to look at things. Children need to feel free to take risks when looking at problems and then discuss various ideas that are possibilities for solving them.

Creativity is a process that leads to the aesthetic.

- It is to innovate pre-existing ideas and understand them in a novel, sometimes inventive, way.

- It is when, rather than simply following directions, we think for ourselves and come up with new ways to look at problems (i.e. science).
- It means that children are using their personal insights and experiences to learn and actively investigate rather than following predetermined steps (i.e. literature).
- It means to think about ideas from other disciplines and use them in new ways (i.e. technology).

Ongoing research indicates that the American workforce will demand graduates who have demonstrated their creativity all throughout their schooling.

How to Encourage Creativity in the Classroom:

- Use brainstorming to generate ideas in all subjects and do not judge them.
- Change up the classroom environment to use space in a different way in order to promote creativity and revive tired minds.
- Expose children to new cultures. This not only broadens students' perspectives, but it also shows them that there is more than one way to approach a situation and to find many solutions.
- Think visually. By organizing, interpreting, and synthesizing knowledge visually, students can see connections and process ideas in new ways.
- Encourage creative synthesis in project-based learning.
- Use technology. Apps for photo editing, sketching, painting, etc. can be used to encourage divergent thinking skills for creative learners to assemble information differently.

"Creativity is a human skill, and the advancement of civilization depends upon it."
–Susan Brookhart in *How to Access Higher Thinking Skills*

Developing Resiliency in Students

Teachers can incorporate resilience-building lessons within the regular curriculum. Resilient qualities flourish in a caring and supportive classroom environment.

- Create a classroom environment where each student feels respected, safe, and cared for—a family that works, plays, and learns together.
- Provide a developmentally appropriate curriculum to meet the needs of the individual child. Integrate the program and curriculum to enable students to see connections to real life situations.
- Structure learning for success—i.e. differentiate instruction to meet the level of the students.
- Goal of <u>independence</u> for the child—the student should take charge of his/her learning.
- Successful learning and mastery leads directly to healthy self-esteem.
- It is important for parents to view their child as competent as per his/her appropriate level of development and ability—e.g. appropriate homework for independence and grading of papers that shows appreciation of student's effort as well as mastery of materials.

Strategies for teaching resiliency in children:

- Reflection: Teach students to reflect upon their learning, i.e. writing—
- How can I improve this?
- What more can I add to my story?
- What motivates the character to act in this story?
- Encourage: Ask questions
- Give answers
- Accept ideas of others
- Legitimize asking for help
- Conference with each student on a regular basis—discuss areas of improvement and/or successes.
- Give immediate feedback as much as possible, i.e. homework, tests, reports, participation, and responses to help the child understand and correct errors. It is more effective to have a student correct homework with the teacher.
- Develop trust. Students need to know and feel that the teacher is a helping person and accepts who he/she is with the goal of guiding to a higher level of learning and living.

Discipline in the Classroom—Responding to Misbehaving

No matter how carefully we teach positive behavior, students will still sometimes misbehave. As they learn to negotiate social expectations, children test limits, get carried away, forget, and make mistakes. Just as when we teach academics, we can use students' behavioral mistakes as opportunities for learning. To do this well, however, teachers must hold on to empathy for the child who misbehaves while still holding her/him accountable. We need to respond to misbehavior in ways that show all of our students that we will keep them safe and see to it that classroom and school rules are observed.

Goals for Responding to Misbehavior

In the *Responsive Classroom* approach to discipline, the overarching goal is to keep focus on learning while maintaining a classroom that's physically and emotionally safe for all. To achieve this, responses to misbehavior should:

- Stop the misbehavior and re-establish positive behavior as quickly as possible.
- Maintain the child's sense of dignity.

- Develop the child's self-control and self-regulation skills.
- Help the child to recognize and fix any harm caused by their mistake.
- Demonstrate that rules help make the classroom a safe place where all can learn.

In classrooms where this approach is used, teachers respond quickly, firmly, and respectfully when a child misbehaves. Minor problems are addressed before behavior gets out of control. Children are held accountable for their behavior while teachers guide their learning so they can make better choices.

Strategies for Responding to Misbehavior

One of the most important things to keep in mind when responding to misbehavior is to address the behavior as quickly as possible. When a child's behavior goes off track, they need immediate feedback from their teacher to help them break their momentum and get back on track. Although this might sound obvious, teachers often let small misbehaviors go, waiting to address them until they've escalated and are much more difficult to reverse.

Three response strategies that are especially effective when used before misbehavior escalates (and that also meet the other goals named above) are 1. Visual and Verbal Cues, 2. Increased Teacher Proximity, and 3. Logical Consequences.

1. Visual and Verbal Cues

Once teachers have modeled expected behaviors and given children opportunities for practice, a visual or verbal cue will often stop a behavior and help a child get back on track.

Simply looking briefly into a child's eyes can powerfully send the message that "I know you know how to do this; now let's see you do it." Other examples of visual cues are a writing gesture for "This is writing workshop; get to work" or a finger against your lips for "Remember, silent lips when someone is sharing."

Verbal cues can be as simple as saying the child's name. Reminding language can also be highly effective: "Sonya, what should you be doing right now?" "Dante, what do our rules say about sharing materials?"

Reminding language works best when a child is just beginning to go off track—about to open a book instead of getting out math materials, or beginning to reach to take a blue crayon away from a tablemate. If, however, the child is well into the undesired behavior, reminding language loses effectiveness. At this point, a clear redirection is needed: "Sonya, put the book away now and get out your math materials." "Dante, choose another color. It's Ellen's turn to use the blue crayon."

2. Increased Teacher Proximity

Sometimes all that's needed to re-establish positive behavior is for the teacher to move next to the child. For example, if the children have been taught how to sit safely in chairs, and Maria has just started tipping her chair back during direct instruction, simply move to stand by Maria or communicate "Sit safely" without drawing undue attention to Maria or disturbing other children. Once Maria sits safely, the teacher's staying nearby for a bit helps the child understand that she must continue to sit safely.

Bringing the child closer, instead of going to the child, is another option. Suppose Darren turns around and begins fiddling with the items on a shelf during Morning Meeting. The class has learned meeting rules, and they also know that their teacher will sometimes direct them to change their seats if they're beginning to misbehave. A quiet "Darren, come sit next to me" brings Darren to his teacher's side in the circle and gets his attention back on his classmates, without breaking the meeting rhythm.

3. Logical Consequences

Logical consequences are another strategy that teachers can use to stop misbehavior while helping children see and take responsibility for the effects of their actions. Logical consequences differ from punishment in that, unlike punishment, logical consequences are relevant (directly related to misbehavior), realistic (something the child can reasonably be expected to do and that the teacher can manage with a reasonable amount of effort), and respectful (communicated kindly and focused on the misbehavior, not the child's character or personality).

Suppose a child scribbles on his/her desk. Having him/her clean the desk would be a relevant, realistic, respectful, and logical consequence. Having him/her miss recess would be irrelevant. Having him/her clean every desk in the classroom after school would also be an unrealistic amount of work, and the uncleanness of the other desks is unrelated to his/her mistake. Saying "You're so rude—you just don't care about anyone but yourself!" would be a disrespectful attack on his/her character.

Introducing the Approach to Children

This approach to responding to misbehavior is most effective when children know in advance what to expect from their teachers. It's important for the teacher to let children know that at one point or another, everyone makes behavior mistakes and needs support to get back on track, and that's okay—just as it's okay to make mistakes when learning an academic skill. It's also important for the teacher to convey the belief that students can and will learn to choose positive behaviors, and that his/her responses to their mistakes will help them do so. Choice of words, along with a friendly, matter-of-fact tone and a few specific examples, will help get this message across. For example, when talking about responses to misbehavior, a teacher might say:

"We're all working on following our classroom rules, but we all make mistakes sometimes. In our class, when you don't follow a rule, it's my job to help you get back on track, fix any problems you caused, and teach you to follow the rule next time. So, for example, if you forget our rule about staying safe and start running and knock down someone's block tower, I might tell you to help them rebuild it."

Or with older students:

"If I see that you are about to break a rule, I may use a signal to help you realize that you are getting out of control. It's not a big deal; it just means you need to check your behavior and get back on track. For instance, I might put my finger on my lips to remind you to be quiet, or I may just say your name and give you a look if I think you know what to do. If I give you a signal like that, I'm giving you a chance to correct your mistake quickly and quietly, without disrupting anyone else's learning."

Knowing Which Strategy to Use

Knowing which strategy to use, and whether more than one strategy is needed, is a skill that comes with practice and depends upon the teacher's knowledge of the children he/she's teaching.

One child who's talking when he/she shouldn't may need only a cue to correct himself/herself. Another child may need a logical consequence for the same behavior. Or the same child may need a cue on one day and a logical consequence on another. Some questions to consider: Which strategy will stop the misbehavior and restore positive behavior as quickly as possible? Which strategy will maintain safety and order for everyone? Which one will help the child develop understanding and self-control? Whichever strategies are chosen, it's important to remember to use them early, just as misbehavior begins. Doing so will prevent problems from mushrooming or becoming entrenched.

Try, Try Again

Responding to misbehavior is one of the most challenging aspects of teaching. Even the most experienced teachers make mistakes. But just as we allow students to make mistakes, we must allow ourselves to make them, too. And then, just as we do with students, we must allow ourselves to try again without judgment, in the spirit of learning to do it better the next time.

ENCOURAGE GOAL SETTING FOR ADVANCED LEARNERS

Give advanced students opportunities to set their own personal learning goals. Display the day's or week's schedule in the classroom. Some advanced learners need to be able to see and process in their mind the sequence of the day's activities; it makes a difference in the way they feel in the classroom. They are often the ones asking, "What's next? What are we going to do today? Now what?" Displaying the schedule enables all students to own their responsibilities for the day and to monitor themselves when they undertake alternative assignments.

All students need experience in setting goals for themselves. Research demonstrates that setting goals has a powerful effect on student confidence and achievements. Advanced learners who come to school overflowing with ideas and energy need to develop the skill to break long-term goals down into smaller, short-term goals that are within their reach. When students set smaller goals that lead to a larger achievement they care about, two things happen: they can focus their energy and ability, which would otherwise become diffused, and they can measure their progress in a tangible way. Perfectionism, a common affliction of high-ability students, becomes more difficult to address in students who lack experience at goal-setting. Instead of "I must write a perfect report," students learn to direct themselves to a more realistic goal: "I must fill out the K-W-L chart on the subject of my report; then, I'll move on to the research."

Executive Functions

The cognitive processes required to plan and organize activities:

- Ability to start and follow through on tasks
- A solid working memory
- Attention span
- Skills at performance monitoring
- Inhibition of impulses
- Goal-directed persistence

Originated in the frontal cortex part of the brain just behind the forehead, the skills begin to develop soon after birth. It takes a full decade or longer to mature.

- Students who are deficient in tasks have trouble getting started on tasks.
- They get distracted easily, lose assignments, and forget to bring home the materials needed to complete homework or forget to hand it in.
- They make careless mistakes because they rush through work or dawdle. They don't know where to begin on long-term assignments and they put off the assignment until the last minute in part due to trouble.
- Their workspaces are disorganized, as well as notebooks, desks, etc.
- In elementary school it is hooked into developmental readiness and given appropriate support for their

immature executive skills. In middle school it all comes to a head due to changing classes and having multiple teachers with diverse expectations.

Teacher expectations

- Teachers need to have a variety of interventions that will depend upon student needs.
- The RTI model is ideal for planning and implementing intervention by the following:

Whole-Class (Tier 1) Interventions	*Small-Group (Tier 2) Interventions*	*Intensive (Tier 3) Interventions*
These strategies can help all students develop executive skills:	*Try these strategies with students who are still struggling after Tier 1 interventions are in place:*	*If Tier 1 and 2 interventions don't help, parents, teachers, and students can work together to develop an individual support plan. Success is more likely if parents, teachers, and students all have specific responsibilities:*

Tier 1	Tier 2	Tier 3
• Establish classroom routines for writing down assignments, for collecting homework, and so on. • Make classroom rules, post them prominently, review them frequently, and role-play how to follow the rules. • Establish electronic information systems in which students and parents can access assignment information and monitor student progress.	• Break the task into parts or make it less open-ended so students will know where to start. • Establish after-school homework clubs. • Provide weekly progress reports to parents. • In small-group coaching sessions, teach students how to plan homework, develop strategies for remembering, and organize their notebooks.	• Define the target behavior and criteria for success. • Identify and implement specific environmental modifications, such as establishing a specific, distraction-free place and time to do homework every day. • Explicitly teach, model and rehearse the needed executive skills regularly. • Have a teacher, parent, or coach check in with the student daily.

Tier 1	Tier 2	Tier 3
• Teach organizational skills, such as how to keep notebooks organized. • Teach students such study skills as how to plan homework sessions and screen out distractions. • Plan fun activities if the whole class achieves certain goals, such as popcorn parties on Friday if eighty percent of homework is handed in on time for the week.	• Institute peer-tutoring programs or train volunteer tutors. • Ask parents to develop an at-home incentive system tied to daily or weekly progress reports • Have students come to the classroom during free time or after school to complete unfinished work.	• Give the student a visual reminder of expectations. • Monitor the student's independent use of the skill over time.

Fostering Healthy Self-Concepts for Teachers

How can teachers foster the development of a healthy self-concept in the students they teach, and in so doing empower those students to move toward responsible citizenship? The following suggestions are offered for consideration by those seeking practical ways to put power and responsibility into the hands of students

First, teachers can see to it that each student in an environment that communicates to him/her that he/she is a person of worth and has ability. Every day, teachers must find some way to say something good to or about students. Some refer to this as being "a good finder." Teachers ought to keep a list of the negative statements made to students—then try each day to reduce this number to zero. Teachers can also list the ways of saying to students "that is good" and then use the list to make the classroom a powerfully positive environment.

Sometimes a teacher may be heard to say, "Now you'd better get busy and quit wasting your time. You never get your assignments done because you waste your time." Instead, a teacher should say, "How can I help you get started?" The teacher can tell students they are good, then watch them try to be. As the cliché goes, "Catch the student doing something good"—then compliment him/her for it. Teachers simply must teach students what it means to have a positive attitude by being positive toward them. Teachers need to let students know that they are special, they are capable, and they are persons of worth. When teachers create a climate that builds up students, they will see the sense of power build in each student. This is practical student empowerment in the classroom.

Second, teachers can model for students that learning and school are sources of enjoyment. So often teachers present a model of difficulty, drudgery, and unhappiness in going about the job of teaching. In research done with secondary students, eighty-five percent of the students surveyed believed that their teachers did not like to teach. If teachers exhibit no enthusiasm for education, they model a demeaning attitude toward learning. If they show no joy in the educational process, they send a strong message to students that learning is not power and that school is only something to be endured until it is over. There is only one way to empower students with the joy that comes from learning and to make learning something to be desired: Teachers must model joy in learning and patiently wait as their behavior is imitated by the students they teach. As students find that learning is enjoyable, their confidence in their own ability to learn will increase. No teacher should disagree with this kind of empowerment—or refuse to empower students by taking this action.

Third, teachers need to see to it that students experience positive reinforcement with sufficient frequency so that they will honestly believe in their ability to succeed. There is power on both sides of the desk. We can strive to make students believe in only us—or we can help them believe in themselves too. Many students feel powerless because they believe that no matter what they do, it will be wrong. That's why a teacher must structure the classroom so that each student can experience some degree of success—and then give recognition for that success. Even the student who appears to have a healthy self-image needs to be reinforced with frequent and specific praise. It is true that some results can be obtained by the use of negative reinforcement, but positive reinforcement has been shown to be more effective and, in the long run, it produces children who feel better and exhibit healthier self-concepts. Feeling positive about oneself is an important part of embracing the power to be self-managing and self-determining. It is a necessity both for making good decisions and taking appropriate action. But just as we individualize instruction in subject areas, we must also approach student empowerment on an individualized basis. Having one standard, one lesson, and one expectation for all students renders some students powerless—automatically. Every teacher, even one who has taught for only a week, should recognize and accept this fact—and be willing to empower students according to their individual needs so they have the best chance to be successful.

Fourth, teachers empower students by communicating that they believe in students and their abilities. They let students know that they have confidence in them and that they trust students' ability to make correct decisions, to do good work, and to succeed at the jobs they are given. Teachers must keep before students at all times the idea "I can do it." Repetition of this thought and reminders of previous successes in school tasks will ultimately empower students to believe in themselves—and to believe in their teachers. The confidence and courage to trust oneself is, in itself, a significant source of power for students. Students who believe they are capable are empowered to be successful. And believing that all students have this power now is wishful thinking. The self-confidence students need to take risks, give effort, fail, recover after a setback, and return with new effort comes from the teacher's confidence in them. Believing "I can do it" is the power needed for success –and the power every teacher must give students if he/she desires a high degree of success.

These are not sophisticated acts of empowerment of students. They are basic. They are fundamental. Yet regardless of the programs we have for empowerment, these actions must be in place. This is our starting point.

We mentioned the fear that teachers have about empowering students—and its impact on the role of the teacher. Enabling students to be empowered does not diminish teacher power. Quite the reverse is true. Teachers do not lose power by building the self-concept of the students they teach. Building up the students they teach, developing strength through healthy self-esteem, and letting students know that they are worthy of confidence serves only to build the power of the teacher along with that of his/her students.

Power, like love, is a strange phenomenon when it exists in human life. Like love, power grows as you give it away. The more you give the more you have. The teacher who gives power to students will see extensions in the power that he possesses. The more the teacher empowers students, therefore, the more power the teacher will have. In the act of empowering students, teachers empower themselves and become enablers of growth for all who are involved. Once administrators help teachers understand these realities and begin to empower students in the four areas we discussed, teachers are apt to see the advantages in advancing to new levels of student empowerment.

Helping Children Reach Their Full Character Potential

Basic Civilities

At the beginning of the year, be sure to:

- Use please and thank you
- Use an adult's last name when speaking to them, e.g., Mr. Jacobson
- Greet people we see at school
- Open doors for others
- Give friends space in line
- Be polite at every opportunity
- Show respect at all times
- Smile

Different Programs

Johnny Appleseed: A Tale of Character (K–1)
Packing our Backpacks for the 5th Grade Journey (3–6)

Learning Equations

Let students calculate the sum of each equation about good character:

- Responsible work ethic + effort = good grades
- Friendship + caring = a happy life
- Honesty + lots of study time = good test scores
- Responsibility + hard work = skill mastery
- Self-respect + integrity = a student of character

Report Card Goal Setting

On the day report cards are to be handed out, each student receives a goal-setting worksheet.

The first part is for predicting what grades the students think they have earned. Use the word earned rather than got. Teachers do not give grades, students earn them.

The second part is recording grades earned in the previous grading period. Report cards are given, and students record the grades that they earned in each subject.

Next, students reflect on whether their grades went up or down, and the reasons for this.

The last step is planning for the future. This involves thinking about our habits and leads to goal-setting for the next grading period. They learn that it is never too late to wipe the slate clean and change their ways.

School Quiet Times

Brainstorm a list of times when students need to remain quiet. Quiet times include:

- During intercom announcements
- When a visitor enters the room
- When a teacher is talking or teaching
- During a test
- In school hallways that adjoin classrooms

Spelling for Character

Weave character into the spelling curriculum.

Select character words to add to the weekly spelling list. Consider these words bonus words for the week.

- For primary grades words like: kind, nice, try, and hope
- For intermediate level, more difficult words, e.g., environment, citizenship, and honesty

Take Five

Five minutes doesn't seem like very much time, but if used well it can help a child feel loved and valued. Find time during the day to connect personally with your students. Make a point to tell each child about something good you see in him or her. This helps children develop the self-respect and confidence necessary for learning.

Student Pledge: What Makes a Good Student?

The Student Pledge:

Respect: I will listen when the teacher is talking and when a classmate is talking.

<u>Responsibility</u>: I will come prepared for class and I will complete and turn in assignments on time.
<u>Caring</u>: I will help my classmates.
<u>Fairness</u>: I will take turns and I will not leave anyone out.
<u>Trustworthiness</u>: I will not cheat, lie, or take things that do not belong to me.
<u>Citizenship</u>: I will be a good role model for younger students in our school.

<u>The Teacher Pledge: What Makes a Good Teacher?</u>

Teacher Pledge:

<u>Respect</u>: I will listen to my students and I will speak in a soft, respectful voice.
<u>Responsibility</u>: I will grade and return papers in a timely manner.
<u>Caring</u>: I will help each student to ask for help.
<u>Fairness</u>: I will treat each student fairly without prejudice.
<u>Trustworthiness</u>: I will honor student confidentiality.
<u>Citizenship</u>: I will be a good role model for my students.

<u>Things to Remember</u>

Change: It is important to remember that change is not a threat, it is an opportunity to learn, grow, and experience the value of your effort.
Mindset: A growth mindset will encourage you to move forward with trying new ideas and approaches to curriculum, and to see children in a way that you have not before.
Creativity: Your creativity is the key to making a change.

Helping to Prevent Peer Rejection

Of all the experiences in values of caring and concern for others that a school can provide, none is more important than a young person's experience of being accepted and valued by a peer group.

Students learn to care about others when they feel cared about themselves. However, when a student feels rejected by peers, both academic learning and world development are impeded. Moreover, students who exclude or tease (bully) peers are damaging their own character development by their insensitivity to the feelings of others.

Friendshipping Skills

Friend goes first
Talk about your friend
Friend chooses what to play
Talk about your friend's topics
Instead of "hogging the ball," take turns
Show you're happy that your friend is happy
Let your friend control his/her half; don't be the "boss"
Be a friendly host; practice meeting the friend's needs
Use the politeness words "please" and "thank you"
Feed the friend; have supervised kitchen fun

Give small, appropriate gifts and share
Friend says when to stop
Do small favors

Important Role of the Teacher

Teachers: Helping Make the Stars Come Out:
Each child is a "star" and each teacher is determined to make the stars come out. When a parent takes a concern to their child's teachers, they can feel confident that it will be resolved—involving an administrator (the Head), principal, etc. if necessary. Teachers want to keep in touch; they will indicate to parents the best times to reach them.

Parent Conferences: The Experts Convene:
The private school benefits children most when it works with parents on a continual basis. Your knowledge of the child and observations are important to share with parents. It is important that this sharing does not only take place at conferences, but in-between as well. Putting the two perspectives together (teacher and parent) completes the total understanding of the child's growth and needs.

Common Goals and Aspirations:
Our community of common interests draws the school together and places our students' differences in a broad and meaningful context. Students respect each other, work and play with each other, learn from each other, and stay in touch with each other long after graduation.

You Are A Character Educator:
You are a character educator. You are helping to shape the character of the children you come into contact with. It's in the way you talk, the behaviors you model, the conduct you tolerate, the deeds you encourage, and the expectations you transmit. For better or worse, you are always doing character education. Be mindful of the values you are always teaching.

Painfully Shy: How You Can Help

Many children and adults in your school could rightly be labeled "shy." These individuals have a healthy interaction with others, but are timid in large groups or with people they don't know well. But when dealing with a person who is painfully shy, care must be exercised. How can you tell if a student or a member of the faculty/staff is more than just shy? The Psychologists in Independent Practice, A Division of the American Psychological Association (APA), lists the following signs of painful shyness:

- Mild chronic low mood, easily embarrassed, low energy
- Failure to initiate social contact
- Frequent sadness, loneliness, or resentment
- Use of alcohol or drugs to reduce social anxiety
- Written work at school exceeds class participation
- Excessive time spent on academic work or solitary professional activity to the exclusion of social interaction
- Little to no expression of anger, sometimes punctuated by angry outbursts

While the root cause of painful shyness can range from stressful life events (e.g., major moves from one school or city to another) to negative family interactions (e.g., frequent parental criticism and shaming to enforce behavioral compliance), stressors can exist in the school environment, too. The APA points to the following stressors:

- Highly competitive, critical, or hostile environments
- Public embarrassment for poor performance
- Dominance behaviors rewarded, and bullying or teasing ignored or encouraged

How Can You Help?

While the school counselor or an outside therapist may be the best person to help an individual suffering from painful shyness, mentors can also play an important role in helping the individual develop confidence in your school environment. For a shy student, the faculty member with whom she/he feels most comfortable is the natural choice. For a member of the faculty/staff, the School Head or Division Head may be in the best position to offer positive feedback.

It may be wise for mentors to consult with the school counselor for training. Additionally, the following tips for mentors from the APA may prove useful:

- Maintain appropriate expectations while communicating empathy for the shy person's painful emotions.
- Encourage them to tell you about their daily experiences and how they feel about them.
- Acknowledge the conflict between the need to belong and fear of rejection.
- Role-play challenging situations with the shy person.
- Help the shy individual set specific, manageable behavioral goals and agreed upon reasonable means to attain them.

- Help challenge the frequent negative thoughts about the self and others, and help them develop constructive alternatives.
- Avoid negative labels and intense pressure for social performance.
- Remember that shyness and social anxiety are common and universal experiences at all ages for most people.
- Tell the person exactly how the specific behaviors of avoidance, passive aggression, or inconsistency affect you, while communicating acceptance of the person.
- Ask for permission to offer constructive feedback (what might be done in the future to achieve favorable outcomes). Approach the shy person when she/he is ready.
- Acknowledge the person's strengths and resources, while communicating warmth and positive feelings toward them.
- Encourage the shy person to be more playful, physically looser, and to practice looking "foolish" while trying new things; do the same yourself. Lighten up, use humor.
- Arrange for shy children to interact with, and mentor, younger children. Encourage group sports, acting, and dancing classes in a supportive environment.

PERSONALIZED EDUCATION

Laurence School is committed to a personalized approach to learning, tailored to each student's individual academic, social, and emotional needs, and throughout each grade assessing those needs. This is the best possible education that can be provided for children and is one of the major strengths that Laurence School offers children and parents.

A Personalized Education:

- Recognizes that differences exist in children in terms of abilities, personalities, learning styles, and maturation
- Understands and takes these differences seriously, and the information is shared with students and parents. The goal is to build on the individual's strengths (verbal, creative, physical, or interpersonal, etc.) and work hard to improve weaknesses. Through positive reinforcement, each student is encouraged to try to do his/her best and take risks in learning.
- Makes an effort to gradually shift responsibility for their own learning to the responsibility of the students
- Starts character education in kindergarten and promotes it continuously throughout the student's entire schooling. Values such as respect, caring for others, responsibility, self-discipline, perseverance, and honesty are considered vital to every child's learning and living.

- Makes ongoing evaluation of each student's progress (socially, emotionally, physically, and academically), which starts in kindergarten and continues through sixth grade. Students' abilities are known quite well during their stay at Laurence School. This makes recommendations for secondary school placement quite meaningful.
- Makes a serious commitment to each child and family. The Laurence School program and approach enables us to have thorough knowledge of our students to date, and an understanding of their potential growth, development, and future needs.

Quotes for Teachers

"In years to come, your students may forget what you taught them, but they will always remember how you made them feel." —Author Unknown

"Better than a thousand days of diligent study is one day with a great teacher." —Author Unknown

"A teacher takes a hand, opens a mind, touches a heart, and shapes the future." —Author Unknown

"To reach a child's mind a teacher must first capture his or her heart." —Author Unknown

"Insanity is doing the same thing over and over again and expecting different results." —Albert Einstein

"Who dares to teach must never cease to learn." —John Colton Davis

"By believing and using strategies for 'The Total Child' approach, you are enabling every child to succeed—academically, socially, emotionally, and physically." —Marvin Jacobson

Reflections

The Importance of Developing Higher Thinking Skills in Students

Children of all ages, starting with kindergarten, need to learn to talk, write, draw, sing, perform, dramatize, etc. These activities can be a creative reflection upon their experience and what the experience means to them.

Every teacher needs to provide regular opportunities for *reflection.* It is known that students learn more effectively if they have to think, talk, or write about their experience in mastering a core subject, telling a story, presenting an oral book report, mastering times tables and other math concepts, as well as making a friend and/or participating in a field trip, community service activity, or sports activity.

Teachers need to prompt students to think about and discuss what they have learned, what has surprised them, what worked well, what problems they encountered, what has helped them solve a problem, why it was important to them, etc.

Reflections Take Many Forms

Keeping a personal journal or learning log is a well known form of reflection. Other forms are personal informal chats (one on one), small group discussions, and letters to a pen pal or friend/relative. Other forms include poems, essays, music, dance, and drawing or other artwork.

Reflections Should be Ongoing

Reflections that are ongoing help children cultivate the habit of thinking and being thoughtful. It doesn't have to use a great deal of class time, i.e., students can take ten to twenty minutes to write in their journals or have discussions, etc. The importance of cultivating the habit is the goal.

Celebrating and Sharing with Others

Celebrations and sharing take the reflection process one step further. As students may invite recognition for their accomplishments, they may encounter new questions, make new connections, and extend their learning.

Student sharing can take various forms. In the most basic kind of sharing, students describe a project (individual or group) and show/tell, e.g. after visiting a homeless center, children might write a group poem or stories that capture insight and feelings about homeless people. The experience of having the Lowman School children visit our campus, and having our sixth grade students host them, is a memorable event that will long be remembered—one that engendered deep feelings of empathy. A written reflection of this event asks students to synthesize what they learned, deepening the learning even more.

Parents, too, can be engaged in helping their children learn how to reflect upon an important family experience/event.

Six Myths About Stress for Teachers

No one will deny it: Working in school environments can be stressful! How can you calm your nerves? And how can you better help students or fellow members of the faculty and staff deal with their own stress? Six myths surround stress, the American Psychological Association reports. Dispelling these myths is the first step in better understanding one's emotions and how to handle them.

Myth 1: Stress is the same for everybody. Completely wrong. Stress is different for each of us. What is stressful for one person may or may not be stressful for another. Each of us responds to stress in an entirely different way.

Myth 2: Stress is always bad for you. According to this view, zero stress makes us happy and healthy. Wrong. Stress is to the human condition what tension is to the violin string: too little and the music is dull and raspy, too much and the music is shrill or the string snaps. Stress can be the kiss of death or the spice of life. The issue, really, is how to manage it. Managed stress makes us productive and happy; mismanaged stress hurts and even kills us.

Myth 3: Stress is everywhere, so you can't do anything about it. Not so. You can plan your life so that stress does not overwhelm you. Effective planning involves setting priorities and working on simple problems first, solving them, and then going on to more complex difficulties. When stress is mismanaged, it's difficult to prioritize. All your problems seem to be equal and stress seems to be everywhere.

Myth 4: The most popular techniques for reducing stress are the best ones. Again, not so. No universally effective stress reduction techniques exist. We are all different, our lives are different, our situations are different, and our reactions are different. Only a comprehensive program tailored to the individual works.

Myth 5: No symptoms, no stress. Absence of symptoms does not mean the absence of stress. In fact, camouflaging symptoms with medication may deprive you of the signals you need for reducing the strain on your physiological and psychological systems.

Myth 6: Only major symptoms of stress require attention. This myth assumes that the "minor" symptoms, such as headaches or acid reflux, may be safely ignored. Minor symptoms of stress are the early warnings that your life is getting out of hand and that you need to do a better job of managing stress.

Successful Teachers

It is not easy to be a teacher! Even though children are naturally curious and want to learn, they:

1. Learn in different ways
2. Think in different ways
3. Understand in different ways
4. Will be at different places in their cognitive, social, emotional, and physical development even though chronologically the same age.
5. Will bring a different set of prior learning experiences and values from their family and community.

Before you, as the teacher, can even begin to instruct your students, it is vital that you build a relationship of TRUST with them. Once that is achieved, a quality instructional program can begin.

Some ways to build TRUST in the classroom:

- Have clear and consistent expectations.
- Make each student know and feel that you care about him/her.
- Establish a time each week to talk with four to five students one-on-one, regarding effort, production, favorite hobbies/interests, weekend activities/ plans, etc.

Other qualities of a Successful Teacher:

- Vibrates with a love for teaching
- Gets to know each student individually
- Learns to structure instruction to the needs of the children
- Differentiates instruction as needed
- Learns to be a counselor in developing a relationship with students
- *"It is the extreme art of the teacher to awaken joy in creative expression and knowledge."* —Albert Einstein

Teacher–Parent Partnership

There is much data from leading child psychologists about child rearing and learning that can help create a positive relationship between parent and teacher.

Some interesting facts are:

- Children spend ninety percent of their time at home and elsewhere and only ten percent at school.
- Children model the values and behavior, including listening skills, of both teachers and parents.
- Parents and teachers need to set limits and allow children to fail as well as succeed, without rescuing them.
- It is ok to say "no" without feeling guilty.
- Children need time and space for reflection and play.
- "Education is a journey, not a race."

Parents and teachers have a similar need to reinforce each other in terms of individual behavior, core values, and shared expectations.

Every child benefits from a positive relationship between his/her parents and teacher.

It is a relationship that builds upon trust and steady positive communication. At the core of this relationship is the love and care we as adults hold dearly for every child. It requires a reservoir of patience, perseverance, and understanding.

In summary, parents and teachers have a partnership with a purpose: namely, the children's lives that we touch every day *and* to make every day important in their character development in elementary school.

TEACHING: A THINKING PROCESS

Clearly, everyone who has ever been engaged in teaching knows that it is a *thinking* process. Effective teaching requires constant evaluation of one's beliefs in light of one's classroom behaviors—and content evaluation of one's behaviors in light of the student outcomes for which one is aiming. Good teachers never reach stasis; they are always striving to "do it" better.

In the past, though, professional development activities were aimed primarily at adding to a teacher's bag of tricks. Today, by contrast, the goal is to revolutionize teachers' entire perspective on how learning occurs. Understanding how the brain works affects curriculum and student learning.

We used to believe that children learned by listening to and mastering what their teachers told them. Now, we have come to see that students construct their own new concepts by testing their established understandings through social interactions, e.g. cooperation learning with others who may or may not endorse those understandings. The goal is to expose students to opposing thoughts of others and help them expand their own.

If classroom practice is ever to reflect this new view of the learning process, classroom teachers must be viewed as the real reformers. And these teachers must have the opportunities to observe colleagues teaching for understanding, to try it out themselves, and then to think and talk about their experiences within a supportive learning community. The Internet has become a tool for all teachers and students, the experienced as well as the new.

Teaching Responsibility

Have Students Rate Their Behavior

Here's a way to help students take responsibility for their own behavior. Post only one rule in your classroom: No student has the right to interfere with the learning of others.

Have students rate their own behavior in a daily class journal. On random days ask students to read their self-ratings aloud. Allow students to challenge one another's self-assessments. Provide rewards for good behavior.

Inappropriate behavior can be handled by establishing a series of steps that allow students to make choices about the consequences of their behavior.

Be A Model of Responsibility in Your Own Classroom

It's important for teachers to model responsible behavior for their students, too. Here are some suggestions:

- Establish a classroom schedule and share it with your students. Include such things as test dates, when special reports are due, and when you will return graded tests and reports. Tell students that they must meet their deadlines, and that you will meet yours.
- When using an overhead projector, laptop computers, or other equipment, demonstrate responsibility by

ensuring that it is handled carefully, used properly, and returned to the media center on time.

- Volunteer to work on school committees, parent groups, and school clubs. Share experiences from these activities with your students, and let them know that acting responsibly results in a feeling of pride at having accepted a job and done it well.

Attendance is a Basic Responsibility

Good attendance is a reflection of student responsibility. Here are some tips for helping students take responsibility for developing good attendance:

- *Demonstrate that you have a positive attitude* toward attendance and productive use of time in class. Showing students that you believe every minute is valuable learning time helps make the idea contagious.
- *Encourage students* (and their parents) to make every effort to schedule doctor, dentist, and other appointments before and after school hours.
- *Refuse to accept excuses* for anything other than legitimate absences.
- *Refuse to view tardiness* as acceptable behavior.
- *When a student must be absent*, make sure he/she understands his/her responsibility to make up any missed work.
- *Talk with students* about the importance of being responsible for one's attendance and the need to develop good work habits and positive attitudes.

Offer Adult Treatment

If a student starts slipping in class academically or in his/her behavior, try calling home and talking to the student about it. Discuss the problem and then let the student know that you think he/she can correct it so you won't have to discuss it with his/her parents.

This technique usually works with older students. They like being treated as responsible people, and they respect the one-on-one conversations with their teacher.

Discuss the approach with parents first so they won't feel left in the dark if they find out you called to talk to their child.

Combine Responsibility and Physical Fitness

Here's how to use an exercise class not only to help students get in shape, but also to make them responsible for sharing what they have learned with younger students:

Once a week, hold a before-school class to teach interested students exercises for younger children. Then schedule several classes each week where the students can act as the teachers. Be sure to continue the weekly training sessions so the student-teachers can learn new routines.

Not only will the students learn responsibility, but they will gain self-confidence and a sense of being in control.

Help Students Set Goals

Students learn responsibility when they learn to set goals and to work toward achieving them. Here are rules to teach students about goal-setting:

- *What should be.* In order to set goals, you need to determine "what is" and then determine "what should be." "What should be" becomes the goal.
- *Measurability.* The "what is" and "what should be" must be measurable by some objective standard.
- *Think big.* There is no excitement in mediocrity. It is a fact that an athlete will perform better against tough competition than against mediocre competition. Set goals that will make you work at your highest level.
- *Work daily.* Become dedicated to reaching your goal. Focus energy on accomplishing.

Talk About Choices

Hold a class discussion about the importance of the choices students make, and about how all choices have consequences. Teachers can show that many behaviors students assume are out of their control are, in fact, choices they choose to make. Here are some examples:

- "*I chose to do my homework.* The result was that I got an 'A' on the test."
- "*I chose to watch a late movie on television.* The result was that I overslept and was late for school."
- "*I chose to spend extra time practicing the violin.* The result was that I won my challenge for second chair."

A discussion of choices can start students thinking about their responsibility for the results of the choices they make.

Use Choice to Teach Responsibility

Granting students choices in school is a powerful way to show respect and confidence in their decision-making ability, to boost their self-esteem, and to teach them responsibility. One very meaningful opportunity for making important and personal choices and for real decision-making is when students misbehave and discipline is needed.

Instead of always doing something to a student offender, next time offer the student the opportunity to take responsibility by doing something to make up for the offense. If the student decides to try to do something of a positive nature—such as providing a service to the class—hold the negative consequences aside.

Consider Cooperative Learning

Cooperative learning is small-group learning that helps teach responsibility through positive interdependence, face-to-face interaction, individual accountability, and interpersonal/small-group skills.

Students learn to take responsibility for staying with the group, helping to complete the group's work, listening to others, sharing material, using names, looking at the speaker, and talking softly.

As students develop responsibility, they will also learn to solve problems, resolve controversy, differentiate ideas, and reach consensus.

Teach Students to Take Responsibility to Resolve Conflicts

A peer mediation program can teach students to take responsibility for resolving their problems themselves rather than resorting to violence.

Mediation sessions are governed by the following rules for students:

- Agree to try to solve the problem.
- Agree to tell the truth.
- Agree not to interrupt.
- Agree not to use name-calling or put-downs.
- Agree not to physically fight.

This system teaches students to take responsibility for handling their own conflicts. The mediation session is set up to preserve or establish respect for individual feelings and needs. Students are given the task of creating workable solutions to their problems.

To begin the process, ask students, "What would you like to see happen to solve this problem?"

Restate the solution each student has offered. If all parties agree, write the settlement down and have each student sign it. If there is no agreement, help the students to negotiate further until they do reach accord.

Experts say students learn responsibility through practice. They must be given responsibility, encouraged to do the right thing—and then be required to live with the consequences of their actions.

Teaching to the Brain

Educators' primary goal is to help students learn. So it may come as a surprise that some experts accuse educators of widely ignoring what is known about the organ of learning—the brain. Experts in brain-based learning claim that traditional instruction is at odds with how the brain learns, and that the typical classroom environment actually inhibits the brain from learning. Schools and teaching should be revamped in light of brain research, they assert.

"There is an enormous amount of very scientific knowledge about the brain," says Leslie Hart, author of *Human Brain and Human Learning*, and a longtime advocate of brain-compatible teaching. Although most brain researchers have studied animals or dysfunctional human brains, their findings still shed light on the normal learning process, he says.

The brain is designed to deal with the confusion of the world around us, Hart explains; it learns by extracting patterns from that confusion. Young children learn to speak by extracting linguistic patterns from the babble of speech they hear, for example.

The brain requires a great deal of input in order to detect patterns. Therefore, educators' attempts to simplify things for students are misguided, Hart believes. "Teachers are taught to present things logically," in neat, step-by-step sequences, he says. This approach produces little learning, however, because the brain "resists logic." Thus, teaching reading, for example, in a logical way—beginning with letter sounds, then moving to consonant blends, and so on—doesn't work very well, he says. An approach that provides more input, such as whole language, works much better.

Fragmenting content is the biggest mistake schools make, says Geoffrey Caine, an education consultant who, with his wife Renate Nummela Caine, a professor of education at California State University, San Bernardino, wrote the recent ASCD book, *Making Connections; Teaching and the Human Brain*. "Teaching bits and pieces has been the focus" of instruction, Renate Caine says. "The brain is looking for meaningful connections; (teachers) actually cut those off" when they reduce learning to memorization of facts that have no personal meaning for the learner.

What teachers should do instead, the Caines advise, is to "orchestrate complex experiences" for students. These experiences should be global and related to real life. To provide them, teachers should use an integrated curriculum, develop ongoing, authentic projects, use grouping and develop a sense of community, and organize instruction around themes.

Student governments and student-produced newsletters, for example, are complex activities through which students can learn subjects such as social studies, grammar, and history, the Caines say. Examples of thematic instruction include devoting a day to teaching fractions in every conceivable context or teaching about the Middle Ages in an interdisciplinary way.

Complex experiences produce better learning, the Caines say, because they become embedded in the students' "locale" memory system, the "autobiographical memory" that records one's ongoing life story—rather than the less efficient rote memory.

Brain-compatible teaching "is everything that education should be," attests Barbara Pedersen of Central Elementary School in Lebanon, Indiana, who practiced it for five years in the classroom and now coaches teachers at fourteen schools in its precepts. The teachers she works with follow five basic principles:

- Provide meaningful content and firsthand experiences, and relate everything to the real world. Students "can't understand the ocean if they don't understand a pond in Indiana," Pedersen says.
- Provide an enriched environment. Teachers bring plants, lamps, and music into their classrooms. They downplay workbooks in favor of field trips and visiting experts.
- Allow adequate time for students to process what they're learning.
- Offer choices in activities. Teachers let students choose whether to write a journal, song, or rap reflecting what they have learned, for example.
- Build trust. Teachers promote active listening and prohibit put-downs.

Although the effort is only in its second year, Pedersen has already seen results. Students are "excited about being here," she reports, and although standardized test scores have not risen, portfolio evaluations "look wonderful."

Downshifting

Brain research also has implications for classroom climate, these experts say.

Human beings are born learners, Hart says. "The brain doesn't need to be motivated to learn any more than the heart needs to be motivated to pump blood." Yet most classrooms actually demotivate students to learn, he asserts.

The prime de-motivator is threat. "School is threatening (to students) from the word go," Hart says, because of the fishbowl atmosphere and teachers' power to assign grades and inflict punishment.

A threatening environment inhibits learning, Hart claims, because threat causes the brain to "downshift" from higher functioning to the more primitive core brain—as when people who are publicly insulted cannot think of a reply, because their facility with language has shut down. The less overt threat of the classroom can produce a similar effect, Renate Caine says, because students are placed in a helpless position. Students should be guided instead of threatened, she advises.

"It's amazing to see how children respond to a non-threatening environment," Hart says. "Everybody blossoms."

Hart's other recommendations for instruction are similar to the Caines'. Teachers should provide students with high levels of input—a profusion of information, experiences, and ideas, he says. Hands-on, real-world experiences should take precedence over the textbook.

Schools must also be freed from the tyranny of the clock, Hart insists, so that students can pursue activities for as long as they find them interesting. He prescribes a "more relaxed and freer atmosphere, with much more choice for the child." Under these conditions, "children will tackle things (teachers) would never have dreamed of assigning them."

Pedersen agrees. "I really believe in brain-based education," she says. "Now that we know there's a better way, we can't just turn our backs on it."

Teaching Values

At Laurence School, we are strongly committed to teaching important values to children. These values are important for children of all ages to learn, honor, and incorporate into their own personality. Our goal is to build self-confidence and respect among all students at Laurence. This has been a long-standing objective and involves sharing and modeling the values of respect, responsibility, caring, and sharing, and having each student practice them at school and home.

We utilize community-building activities such as morning meetings, weekly assemblies, community service, and active and on-going communication with parents to help facilitate this instruction. It also involves a very clear way of dealing with students' emotions and listening carefully to him/her without judgment. Positive language and clear, respectful communication are the keystones. The method validates feelings while offering students safe ways to express strong emotions and to help them decide on how to resolve them through choices. Our faculty supports this approach and works hard to make it part of the fabric of the school. The result is that at Laurence our students feel secure, self-confident, and respected.

Respect is the way one talks to and acts toward others, and sometimes it means following the rules. Children need to learn about respecting people and need to learn to understand that being respectful is one of the ways they acknowledge another person. Respect means treating people the way you want to be treated. They also need to understand that respect is one of life's important values now and when they "grow up." Implicit in demonstrating respect is understanding what needs to be done in a certain situation. It is truly a complicated concept that is hard for many adults to practice.

By demonstrating and modeling the importance of values every day, the children at Laurence begin to integrate these concepts into who they are. These lessons are a vital part of their growth and development in the "Total Child" concept.

The R Program

Everyone has heard of the 3 R's—reading, 'riting, and 'rithmetic—but there are other important words beginning with the letter "R" that can affect the total atmosphere of the school or classroom.

These "R" words include student rights, respect, responsibility, rules, doing what is right, reputation, and recognition.

Below is a brief synopsis of what we share regarding each "R" word:

Rights: Each student has the right to learn, be happy, and to receive a good education in our school.

Respect: The Golden Rule. Treat others as you would like to be treated. Develop a good feeling of caring for and about others and their feelings.

Responsibility: Teachers have the responsibility of teaching everyone in their classroom everything they need to know to succeed in that grade and to enter the next grade. Students have the responsibility of trying to learn everything that is taught. They do this by responding to the teacher's questions, participating in discussions, and showing their understanding of material by completing assignments. Asking for help and taking risks is an important part of learning.

Rules: Students have to know how to play by the rules. Knowing and following the rules allows them to succeed in school. We stress the importance of everyone in the school playing by the same rules.

Doing what is Right: We assume that everyone knows right from wrong. All students are encouraged to try to make the right choices. During this part we use many examples, such as the importance of telling the truth, of not taking things that don't belong to you, of supporting a friend even if it means others will not approve, etc.

Reputation: We discuss the importance of projecting a good image and of knowing what others think of you, your class, or your school. We stress that reputation is based on behavior and how one treats others.

Recognition: When someone does something well, teachers recognize the accomplishment with grades, reinforcements, and/or positive comments. Teachers are encouraged to send notes home for additional recognition.

The "R" program is open-ended. Students and teachers are encouraged to come up with other meaningful "R" words, such as remember, recycle, recess, or restroom.

The "R" words are "catch" words. Teachers can use them to remind or reprimand.

They are simple enough that students know what they mean and how to apply them, and we have found that they work much better than negative remarks.

Thoughts for Teachers

Think deeply about your roles as teachers, and about the personal qualities and caring you bring to the classroom.

Diligently plan for how you will develop caring relationships and a sense of community in your classrooms—how you will make certain every single student feels that their worth and dignity is valued and affirmed.

Include in your array of best practices effective strategies for weaving character development across your curriculum.

Highlight values in your daily lessons or plan service-learning activities to give students opportunities for real life learning experiences.

And, perhaps most important, involve students in creating a caring classroom rooted in excellence, respect, and responsibility through active participation in morning meetings, class meetings, and creating a class constitution to be a learning document to refer to often.

A very important way students learn good character is by experiencing the way the teacher treats other students, their teaching style, personality, and how they address ethical issues as they inevitably arise.

Character education needs to be continuously worked into the fabric of everyday life in each and every classroom, playground, enrichment or specialist class, etc.

It's important to pay attention to the relationship you are building with your children.

Be honest; don't shade the truth with them.

Be fair, consistent, and firm while explaining the reasons behind your actions.

All ages of children need adult guidance about what is right and what is wrong.

Remember, children need you as models, not parents.

You don't need to be perfect or infallible. When you are wrong, admit it! Just try to make sure this doesn't happen too often!

It is important to remember that change is not a threat; it is an opportunity to learn, grow, and experience the value of your effort.

A growth mindset will encourage you to move forward with trying new ideas and approaches in your curriculum; it will help you to look at children in ways that you have not done or seen before.

I know that connecting individually with students is one of the most powerful ways to support all students emotionally, socially, and academically.

Your creativity is the key to making change.

What Did You Learn in School Today?

Perhaps the question asked most often, after "How are you?" is "What did you learn in school today?" All too frequently, the response is a grunt or the retort of "nothing." But we all know it's unlikely that a person who was awake could experience an entire day without learning a single thing. The real message being communicated is probably "I haven't thought about it yet" or "You wouldn't understand."

Perhaps we are posing the question to the wrong person—the student. It might be more telling if we asked ourselves as teachers or administrators "What did we learn in school today?" Have you ever thought about this? Did you give yourself a chance to consider what you've learned? Will it change your behavior tomorrow? From whom did you learn it? How could you have learned more?

Schools are good places in which to learn things. They have all the needed fixtures, like desks and computers. They have good people, too, like students, teachers, aides, and administrators. Those of us who have spent most of our lives in these places should be brilliant. Maybe we just need to spend more time considering what it was that we learned today—or this week or this semester.

Did we learn to be a better listener? Did we learn how to access the Internet almost as quickly as a sixth grader? Did we learn that "being first might be worst?" Did we learn that problems are opportunities, and that solving problems is what really makes us essential? Did we learn that being right isn't as important as doing right?

What will you tell your spouse, your children, or your friends when they ask, "What did you learn in school today?"

What We Learn

We learn:

- 10% of what we read
- 20% of what we hear
- 30% of what we see and hear
- 70% of what is discussed with others
- 80% of what we experience personally
- 95% of what we teach someone

Chapter Five
What I Believe In

Technology

We live in a global economy increasingly driven by consumer demand for technology.
Today's students must be prepared, unlike any other generation before, to think critically and analytically while engaged with innovation and creativity.

Children need to be guided by parents and teachers to find the most positive ways to utilize all that technology has to offer. Indeed they have grown up in an unusual world that technology provides, but there are a lot of the many aesthetic experiences that are awaiting them as they dream about what is and what might be if we dream, imagine, and create.

After extensive research and many years of observing children as they learn and master information, I have been able to see the value of integrating technology on all levels of how children learn. It has become an increasingly essential tool to enhance all types of learning in the twenty-first century.

Since technology has become part of the daily lives of parents, children model their style of life as they move through the paces of going to school and participating in many activities where technology plays a significant role in providing powerful learning experiences, content and resources, and authentic meaning to stimulate learning.

Teachers need to be continually exposed and trained in appropriate use of technology in every classroom. Starting in kindergarten (iPads) through sixth grade when more complicated apps are used in school as well as at home.

Outside of school, many students' lives are filled with technology that provides information and resources 24/7. It is powerful to have access to and participate in social networks, freedom to pursue areas of passion in their own way and own pace. It opens up a whole new world where people from all over the world share ideas, collaborate, and learn new things.

The Importance of Teaching Digital Citizenship

Internet safety requires ongoing vigilance since children are still not aware enough to know that if they use it to have "fun" at the expense of another, it is totally not acceptable at school as well as at home. Therefore, parents of school-age children need to be aware of the danger of using social networking, and that it can be hurtful and damaging to friends or others if used improperly.

At school we are careful to select age-appropriate apps for all areas of the curriculum so children will feel the power of self-selection and diversity of something new and different. However, I hope that books will always be a major resource to them, and technology will provide supplementary information.

Through the use of technology and online learning, we a have a platform for innovation for children. Since every child has his/her own style of learning, we can personalize learning to meet individual needs. It enables schools and teachers to deliver high quality technology and learning experiences anytime, anywhere. We live in a time where technology can offer education a great deal.

Dreaming, Thinking, and Technology

At times, nostalgia can bring us back in time to memories that fill us with joy, happiness, and hope. Even though technology and social media are now all-pervasive, important experiences of the past are still good for the soul and a reminder that life is with people and kindness is "king."

Today's world is more complex and visually oriented. The simpler things like reading a book and holding and smelling the print are being replaced by e-readers and the like. Communication has been reduced to email and texting, speaking to someone face to face on the telephone is becoming obsolete. With all the excitement that technology is providing via TV, movies etc., perhaps the old days when people spoke to one another with eye contact, and when reading need not to provide instant gratification e.g.—looking around at the trees and imagining what pictures in the mind might look like to stimulate creativity. It is important to take time to think and dream without needing the visuals and enjoy the important experience of visualizing in one's own mind (where deep thinking takes place).

Dreaming is healthy for children and adults, and dreamers are known to make things happen for themselves if they continue to pursue their dream.

LAURENCE SCHOOL MOVING FORWARD

Reflections of Six Decades

As the weights of justice are aligned to achieve a balance, education must also aim for and attain this ideal. Since its inception in 1953, Laurence has successfully balanced the educational diet—tending to nurturance, maturation, and application of the mind and body, thus setting the foundation to help students become contributory participants in society. Our approach aims to provide a balance in curriculum through a well-organized academic program and enrichment through science, social studies, the fine arts, foreign language, computer education, character development, and community service focusing on all people and all cultures that make up our great mosaic, USA. Laurence has emerged as a pioneer in the field of education and inspired a vast range of interests. Our key to fully developing the inner strength and tapping the aptitude of the individual student is to treat the child as the unique individual that he/she is. This individuality is not exclusive. Recognizing the individual needs of each student is combined with helping him/her utilize the group process to its fullest. In our classrooms, usually numbering between fifteen and twenty-two pupils per class, our professional staff can evaluate and plan for the students' rate and style of learning through ability grouping in math and reading. Neither is the accelerated student unchallenged nor the student with learning differences rushed.

At Laurence, we emphasize not merely learning, but a method of learning based upon current research to offer our children ways to be creative and meet their needs. There are five goals that are continually interwoven into our teaching fabric: (1) Active participation of every student in learning and social responsibility (2) Critical and creative thinking and problem solving (3) Mastery of academic subjects (4) Make learning fun, exciting, and applicable to everyday life (5) Look toward and prepare students for future challenges.

In projecting our growing needs we have created a beautiful and wonderful campus of five acres. Our landscaping includes a grassy, regulation size ball field fully equipped and used for kindergarten play to upper grades for team sports. Our campus has been called an oasis, Shangri-La, and heaven for all children to learn and grow.

Our basic philosophy is that a student learns not by rote memorization of facts, but by experiencing the reality of a subject in its diverse forms, connecting subject matter through music, art, computers, science, and social studies to create meaningful learning. In continuing to meet the needs of all students and parents, we move forward by offering an environment of moral, academic, and enriched learning that meets the needs of all students. As children learn to accept and appreciate themselves, they are able to experience the acceptance of other people and cultures, thus instilling within themselves the values of caring and concern for all in our multicultural society. This surely contributes to healthy social and emotional growth for the Total Child. Our goal is to continue to seek the very best for our children as they develop into healthy and productive human beings.

The approach to the Total Child has been proven by the test of time.

Found Poetry

Dear Mr. & Mrs. Jacobson,
We started writing you a letter in class, but it didn't turn out the way we expected it to. Instead of a letter, when we put our words and phrases together we found we had written a poem...

Found Poetry
Holding Hands With a Smile, Brightening Up the Day!

You work so hard and I honor you.
Whenever I get a hug from you, I feel like I'm being hugged by a hero.
The truth is, I would like to be with you all day every day.
You make my heart blossom.
Because you were always here for me,
I have so many compliments and memories to share with you.
You are so dependable and loving.
When I see you, I feel overjoyed.
When I see you, I feel safe and encouraged.
You are the ones who make our school beautiful.
It's challenging to describe you two, but I think you are superb.
You are brilliant, creative, and generous.

You invented the outstanding school we go to; you can do anything.
You guys are so so so (you get the point) inspiring.
You are in great shape!
I feel the enormous love and care that Mr. and Mrs. Jacobson put into me.
Mr. and Mrs. Jacobson can brighten up a sad moment.
In a crowd of a million, I could easily find Mr. and Mrs. Jacobson
because they are so special.
When Mr. and Mrs. Jacobson see you and give you a marvelous hug,
it lights up your hear, eyes, and all of your body.
My days at Laurence are perfect and sublime—I couldn't, and wouldn't,
think of anyone better than Mr. and Mrs. Jacobson.

Out of your hearts, sprang Laurence!

Thank you for inspiring us and sending us smiles. Thank you for making us feel precious. You understand us and we appreciate you. You are our favorites, our friends, our Founders.

With much love,
House 3B

Fiftieth Year—What I Love About Laurence

A Sampling of Personal Notes Over the Years From Parents and Students

April 16, 2015

Dear Mr. and Mrs. Jacobsen & Laurie,

I am still downloading the flood of emotions I felt visiting Laurence today. It seems like yesterday that I first walked into the office at Laurence at the age of 6. I was greeted by a friendly gentleman who knelt down to introduce himself. His words were soft and kind and I remember feeling instantly comfortable in this new place. It became my second home for the next 6 years of my life. I learned how to be kind here, what it meant to learn and create, what friendship meant, what being responsible was, and most importantly what it meant to be loved and nurtured by people other than my family.

Today, 30 years later, I was greeted by the same face, the same gentle voice, and reintroduced to the same principles that are so deeply a part of who I am today. I realized I felt so at home today because I was home. Yes it is upgraded, current, cutting edge and amazingly so. But at the heart of everything that I heard and saw, it's the very same place that I was lucky enough to be a part of so many years ago. I left feeling such a strong pride in the school and also a powerful reminder that wonderful education does nurture the human mind and spirit in the most important way.

Visiting Laurence again made me truly excited for the next phase in my daughter Eden's life and education. Knowing that there are people who care so deeply about children thriving in an educational environment is so reassuring as a parent. The magical part of today for me was that these people are not strangers.

What an incredible legacy and gift your family has shared with so many children and their families. I am grateful beyond words that I was one of those children.

Love,
Lauren Born

5/2015

Dear Marvin and Lynn,

Thank you for another wonderful year at Laurence. I especially want to tell you what an honor and a privilege it has been to help lead the way through the many celebrations honoring the school's 60th anniversary—and the two of you. You both have become very special to my family and from the bottom of our hearts we are grateful to have you in our lives. I saw this piece and for some reason it immediately made me think of you. You have given so much of yourselves over the years to countless kids and families and have touched many hearts and souls. I hope that you will look at this and be reminded of the 'three hearts' you've touched in my family.

Thank you with much love and gratitude,

Barb, Randy & Jolie

July 14, 2015

Dear Mr. Jacobson,

As Alec is getting ready to start 3rd grade, we wanted to take a moment to clearly convey to you our sincere appreciation for your commitment to the well being of each individual child. It seems a lot of schools and educators may give that concept lip service but we feel Laurence really means it – and genuinely cares on a personal level. Since your observation of Alec's transitional issues at the end of Kindergarten and start of 1st grade, we have seen so much progress – academically and socially. Your suggestion to seek guidance, and the subsequent efforts of the teaching staff to implement a plan and find specific ways to help Ale learn better, have proven invaluable. We are thrilled that he has experienced such an amazing cognitive spurt and has gained so much confidence. His progress reports consistently improve – we love seeing all the "E"s nowadays. He, and we, consider Laurence a second home, and we are incredibly pleased with the education Laurence provides.

You are, and will always be, appreciated for the work you have done and continue to do. Each child has potential – but Laurence students are so fortunate to attend a school so ready and able to help children realize that potential. Thanks again.

Best,
Nancy & Narb A

December 11, 2013

Dear Mrs. and Mrs. Jacobson,

I enjoyed having the opportunity to share a special brunch with our families. I feel privileged that Treven has grown to be a kind and capable young man and that it is his life and development that is central to our bond.

You presented an unexpected and treasured gift that certainly highlighted my awkwardness, though I am thoroughly enjoying this feeling now. I have marveled at the thought, care, attention to detail, artwork and the chirography (I love that word yet rarely get to use it.) Your dedication, time and effort to organize the process involving so many others to assemble and complete this as a book gave a simple story a remarkable life.

Life is precious , and our relationships are built not on what we do, but who we are. Your care certainly echoes that, and I can carry with me a fond regard for how special you are to so many people -- and just to me. Your kindness and support including me and my family has created a warm, loving place I can draw from

Thank you again for your kind, very special and surprising gift.

Lee

February 9, 2011

Dear Mr. Jacobson,

I learned many important lessons from you over the years and it's hard to know just how many of my core beliefs regarding children, education and the world are yours or my own.

At the top of the list, has to be the importance of educating the total child. The value of this philosophy has become even more important over the years as we are bombarded by more and more information fighting for our cognitive attention. Being a good person involves more than being smart or doing well at school. It is not mutually exclusive, but is part of more important whole.

"Don't change how you do things because of a few loud and angry comments" was your advice that helped bring perspective to my personal and professional life. Not being strong or demonstrative enough in my way of doing things, I wavered at any slight sign of criticism or complaint. I have learned over the years to be a good listener, to validate and take in information, even when it is given forcefully, and to evaluate it thoroughly before coming to a decision regarding a practice or policy. This has helped me innumerable times.

When Brian was having his trouble in 5th grade, and I was berating myself for not being a better parent, you shook me to my core when you firmly told me that 'this wasn't about me.' That advice allowed me to focus on the real issues and to make a positive impact in my son's life. Your direction kept me focused as we battled to keep this child emotionally healthy and mentally stable.

I don't have a great memory, but these three lessons you taught me have stayed with me and are never too far below the surface of my being.

Thank you for your wisdom and your friendship over the years. I very much look forward to getting an autographed copy of your book!

Janice

Thursday, March 25, 2010

Dear Mr. and Mrs. Jacobson,

You are two absolutely wonderful, outstanding and amazing people! Your presence and focus and commitment and concern toward each and every child in your care and in our Laurence Community is not only a blessing but it is also an incredible treasure for us all.

Tracey and I wanted to be sure to say a special thank you for being there in an extraordinary way for Strauss today. You are always 'there' for the children and today was an immeasurably important moment during which your presence was more than appreciated.

We love you, respect you and cherish the amazing opportunity to be a part of your lives, family and community.

With deep gratitude, profound affection and the utmost admiration,
Sincerely
Richard and Tracey C

April 16, 2015

Dear Mr. and Mrs. Jacobsen & Laurie,

I am still downloading the flood of emotions I felt visiting Laurence today. It seems like yesterday that I first walked into the office at Laurence at the age of 6. I was greeted by a friendly gentleman who knelt down to introduce himself. His words were soft and kind and I remember feeling instantly comfortable in this new place. It became my second home for the next 6 years of my life. I learned how to be kind here, what it meant to learn and create, what friendship meant, what being responsible was, and most importantly what it meant to be loved and nurtured by people other than my family.

Today, 30 years later, I was greeted by the same face, the same gentle voice, and reintroduced to the same principles that are so deeply a part of who I am today. I realized I felt so at home today because I was home. Yes it is upgraded, current, cutting edge and amazingly so. But at the heart of everything that I heard and saw, it's the very same place that I was lucky enough to be a part of so many years ago. I left feeling such a strong pride in the school and also a powerful reminder that wonderful education does nurture the human mind and spirit in the most important way.

Visiting Laurence again made me truly excited for the next phase in my daughter Eden's life and education. Knowing that there are people who care so deeply about children thriving in an educational environment is so reassuring as a parent. The magical part of today for me was that these people are not strangers.

What an incredible legacy and gift your family has shared with so many children and their families. I am grateful beyond words that I was one of those children.

Love,
Lauren Born

Resources

American Association of School Administrators
http://www.aasa.org
The Educating the Total Child advocacy campaign

American Journal of Public Health
Downey, Doug, Sociologist
Ohio State University/Indiana University
Study on growth rates of Kindergarten & 1st Grade body-mass indexes

American Psychological Association (APA)
Division of Psychologists in Independent Practice
ISM Update for School Heads Vol. 6, No 6
February 14, 2008

ASCD (formerly the Association for Supervision and Curriculum Development)
http://www.ascd.org
Educational Leadership
September 2005 Volume 63 Number 1
The Whole Child Pages 8–13
What Does It Mean to Educate the Whole Child?
The Whole Child Pages 20–24
Unconditional Teaching

Baumrind, Diana, Psychologist
on being an Effective Parent of an adolescent

Bickart, Toni S. and Syvil Wolin
Practicing Resilience in the Elementary Classroom
PRINCIPAL Magazine
November 1997
Pages 21–23

Bleifield, Carol, School Counselor
on being an Effective Parent of an adolescent

Brody, Jane F.
Personal Health
NY Times
February 10, 2010

Brown, Nacio Herb
"*Good Morning*" (1939 song) used in the 1952 musical film
Singin' in the Rain

Caine, Geoffrey Education Consultant
Caine, Renate Nummela
Professor of Education California State University—San Bernardino
Making Connections: Teaching and the Human Brain
ASCD

A Caring School Community
http://www.devstu.org/caring-school-community
(K–6 program)
Class Meetings
Cross-age Buddies
Family Involvement Activities

Channing Bete Company
PATHS
Promoting Alternative Thinking Strategies
http://www.channing-bete.com/prevention-programs/paths/paths.html
Identify wide range of feelings
Calming oneself through breathing techniques
Learn to understand others perspectives by using 11 step model to solve problems
Listen, organize, plan, pay attention and set academic goals

Committee for Children
Second Step (Social Skills for Early Childhood & Violence Prevention)
K–9 curriculum
http://www.cfchildren.org/second-step.aspx
Confessore, Nicholas
Tramps Like Them
Charles Murray Examines the White Working Class in "Coming Apart"
The New York Times Sunday Book Review
February 10, 2012

Dawson, Peg, Psychologist
Center for Learning and Attention Disorders
Portsmouth, New Hampshire
pegdawson@comcast.net
Smart but Scattered: The Revolutionary "Executive Skills" Approach to Helping Kids Reach Their Potential with Richard Guare
(Guilford Press, 2009)
Executive Skills in Children and Adolescents: A Practical Guide to Assessment and Intervention
(2nd ed., Guilford Press, 2010)
Educational Leadership October 2010

De Bello, Thomas D. and Richard J. Guez
How Parents Perceive Children's Learning Styles
PRINCIPAL Magazine
November 1996
Pages 38–39

Dewey, John
Philosopher, psychologist, educational reformer

Dweck, Carol, Ph.D.
MindSet

Erickson, Erik Psychologist
Childhood & Society
Developmental Stages, Tasks & Learning of Children's Psycho-Social Development

Evans, Robert
Family Matters

Feiler, Bruce
Overscheduled Children: How Big a Problem
The New York Times
www.nytimes.com
October 11, 2013

Ginott, Haim G., Psychologist
Between Parent and Child by
New Solutions to Old Problems
The Macmillan Co. NY
13th printing 1967
pp 144-46

Goleman, Daniel
Emotional Intelligence
Greenspan, Stanley I.
Building Healthy Minds

Hallowell, Edward J.
Driven to Distraction

Harvey, Virginia Smith
Raising Resiliency Schoolwide
From Principal Leadership
THE EDUCATION DIGEST
March 2007
Pages 33–39

Harper, Susan
Newspaper article
January 2011

Independent School Management
http://isminc.com/
"Painfully Shy: How Can You Help?"
ISM Update for School Heads
Vol. 6, No. 6 2/14/08

Mosher, Joy Dr., Professor Education
The Fourth and Fifth Rs
Respect and Responsibility
Children's Literature and Character Development
Volume 8, Issue 1 Fall 2001
Center for the 4th and 5th Rs
Education Department
SUNY Cortland
P.O. Box 2000
Cortland, NY 13045
www.cortland.edu/c4n5rs/
http://www2.cortland.edu/dotAsset/199292.pdf

PACE Program (for cognitive efficiency & fluency)
The Brain Trainers
http://www.thebraintrainers.net/
Perry, Bruce D. M.D., Ph.D.
Resilience: Where Does it Come From?
SCHOLASTIC EARLY CHILDHOOD TODAY Magazine
October 2002
Pages 24–25

Pedersen, Barbara
Teacher Coach in Brain-compatible Teaching
Central Elementary School
Lebanon, Indiana

Pink, Daniel
Former White House speech writer for Vice President Al Gore
"A Whole New Mind"

P.J. the Spoiled Bunny by Marilyn Sadler

Santa, Anne
How Children Develop Resiliency
INDEPENDENT SCHOOL Magazine
Spring 2006
Pages 66–70

Seattle Childrens Development Program Research
http://www.seattlechildrens.org/
Seattle Children's Hospital
P.O. Box 5371
Seattle, WA 98145-5005

Stone,Susan C. J.A., M.F.C.C.
Children and Stress
Beverly Hills, CA

Swanson, David Ph.D.
"The Healthy Child'
Quarterly Free Newsletter
January 21, 2009

Swick, Kevin J. and Nancy Y. Freeman
Nurturing Peaceful Children to Create a Caring World
CHILDHOOD EDUCATION Magazine
Fall 2004
Pages 2–8

The Diary of a Young Girl by Anne Frank

To Kill a Mockingbird by Harper Lee

Willlis, Scott
Teaching to the Brain
ASCD
Hart, Leslie
Human Brain and Human Learning

The Full Circle Family Foundation
CHARACTER Newsletter Summer 2001
Center for Advancement of Ethics and Character

Epilogue—Hope

There are several thoughts that have motivated me throughout my life:

Optimism isn't just a shift in perspective. It is an act of bravery and courage.

Change is not a threat, it is an opportunity to learn and grow.

What you allow, you encourage.

Vision without action is merely a dream.
Vision and action create progress.

Both children and adults need nourishment, attention, respect, and guidance in order to reach their potential.

And probably the most influential of them all...

Of all the forces that make for a better world, none is so powerful as hope. With hope one can think, one can work, and one can dream. If you have hope, you have everything.

Hope inspires children to think, learn, dream, and move forward as they grow and develop with the potential to contribute to a better world. This is the key that makes all things possible.

Nowhere is this expressed better than in the following poem by my son:

Hope

To stand up straight
When your back folds over
When knees weaken
When tears run down your cheeks
To look forward Out of the Gloom
To see the trees, flowers, roses, plants
All in bloom in the Sun
Hope is the sun
Or else the sun would not rise
Each morning it would be swallowed up
By the ocean forever
But the sun does rise
Each morning the rays light up the world
And then the sun peeps over the mountaintop
To begin a new day.

A new day to love and to live
Not always in the darkness of night
But to love and to live and to smile

In the eve the sun drops into the ocean
There is night
It is cold and dark
It takes the sun inside of us to bring joy
To run and laugh to experience love

It must come and will come
By our pushing for hope
For daylight shall overcome night.

–Greg Jacobson, Age 12

Global Learning

Acknowledgements

While compiling, editing, and proofing the pages of this book, it became clear to us that Mr. Jacobson truly embodies the definition of SUCCESS as defined by Robert Louis Stevenson:

Who Is A Success?

That man is a success who has lived well,
laughed often and loved much;
who has gained the respect of intelligent
men and the love of children;
who has filled his niche and
accomplished his task;
who leaves the world better than he
found it, whether by an improved poppy,
a perfect poem, or a rescued soul;
who never lacked appreciation of
earth's beauty or failed to express it;
who looked for the best in others
and gave the best he had.

Mr. Jacobson has truly touched the lives of so many children, parents, and educators and leaves the world in a better place than when he found it.

May the strength of his legacy through Laurence School and his words within this book be a source of professional pride and personal accomplishment to him.

We are proud to have played a small role in helping him to achieve this written compilation of his contribution to early childhood education and his thoughts and words to families over the years.

He continues to be an inspiration to those who are fortunate to know him.

Sincerely,
Patti Claybourne, Janice Lang, and Pat Orland

www.ingramcontent.com/pod-product-compliance
Lightning Source LLC
Chambersburg PA
CBHW060745100426
42813CB00032B/3404/J

* 9 7 8 1 9 4 4 0 3 7 3 9 0 *